JUSTICE

NOW!

HOSEA
AMOS
MICAH
in Today's English Version

With Helps for Reading and Understanding

Parish Life Press   Philadelphia

5741D76   Printed in U.S.A.   16-450

Contents

Preface v

Today's English Version
   Hosea 1
   Amos...23
   Micah 43

Helps for Reading and Understanding
  1. The Word of the Lord Came.................... 61
  2. Love and Responsibility 69
  3. Accountability 78
  4. Here, There, and Everywhere 82
  5. Judgment Now...86
  6. Then Comes the Morning 91
  7. All in the Balances....................................96
  8. Beginning at Home 103
  9. The All-Seeing Eye 109
 10. Tears and Trouble 115
 11. Ruin and Restoration 121
 12. A Case in Point..126
 13. The Time Is Now.....................................131

PREFACE

THE PROPHETS OF ANCIENT ISRAEL were primarily spokesmen for God. They not only spoke about the future, but also recalled the lessons of the past, and probed the meaning of the present for God's people. Often their awareness of the will of God led them to challenge the civil and religious establishment of their day.

The prophets spoke in vivid images taken from the experiences of everyday life, such as farming and sheep raising, the weather, marriage, warfare, and building. Their messages have survived because they turned out to be profoundly true. The disaster they saw coming took place. But even more important, God's people survived, as the prophets also foresaw would happen. Much of what they said, in spite of its ancient setting and imagery, has a distinctly relevant sound today.

Amos was the first prophet in the Bible whose message was recorded at length. He preached to the people of the northern kingdom of Israel about the middle of the eighth century B.C. It was a time of great prosperity, notable religious piety, and apparent security. But Amos saw that prosperity was limited to the wealthy, and that it fed on injustice and on oppression of the poor. Religious observance was insincere, and security more apparent than real. With passion and courage he preached that God would punish the nation. He called for justice to "flow like a stream," and said, "Perhaps the Lord will be merciful to the people of this nation who are still left alive."

Hosea, who also preached in the northern kingdom, appeared a few years after Amos. He was especially concerned about the idolatry of the people and their faithlessness toward God. Hosea boldly pictured this faithlessness in terms of a disastrous marriage—his own! Just as his wife Gomer turned out to be unfaithful to him, so God's people had deserted the Lord. For this, judgment would fall on Israel. Yet in the end God's constant love for his people would prevail, and he would win the nation back to himself and restore the relationship. This love is expressed in some of the most moving words of Scripture: "How can I give you up, Israel? How could I abandon you? My heart will not let me do it! My love for you is too strong."

Micah, who appeared shortly after Hosea, was from a country town in Judah, the southern kingdom. He was convinced that Judah was about to face the same kind of catastrophe that Amos had predicted for the northern kingdom, and for the same reasons. Micah's message, however, contains more clear and notable signs of hope for the future. Passages especially worth noting are the picture of universal peace under God (4.1-4); the prediction of a great king who would come from the family line of David and bring peace to the nation (5.2-4); and, in a single verse (6.8), the summary of much that the prophets of Israel had to say: "What the Lord requires of us is this: to do what is just, show constant love, and humbly obey our God."

Like the New Testament in *Today's English Version,* this is a distinctively new translation that does not conform to traditional vocabulary and style. It seeks to express the meaning of the Hebrew text in words and forms accepted as standard by people everywhere who employ English as a means of communication.

Where there is general agreement that the Hebrew text cannot be translated as it now stands, the translation employs the evidence of other ancient texts or follows present-day scholarly consensus. All such modifications are identified in footnotes. Other footnotes give information designed to help the reader understand the meaning of the text, especially where ancient beliefs are expressed or alluded to.

HOSEA

1 This is the message which the Lord gave Hosea son of Beeri during the time that Uzziah, Jotham, Ahaz, and Hezekiah were kings of Judah, and Jeroboam son of Joash was king of Israel.

Hosea's Wife and Children

² When the Lord first spoke to Israel through Hosea, he said to him, "Go and get married; your wife will be unfaithful, and your children will be as bad as she is. My people have left me and become unfaithful."
³ So Hosea married Gomer, the daughter of Diblaim. She became pregnant and bore him a son. ⁴ The Lord said to Hosea, "Name him 'Jezreel,' because it will not be long before I punish the king of Israel for the murders that his ancester Jehu committed at Jezreel.*a* I am going to put an end to Jehu's dynasty. ⁵ And at that time, in Jezreel Valley, I will destroy Israel's military power."
⁶ Gomer had another child, and this time it was a girl. Then the Lord said to Hosea, "Name her 'Unloved,' because I will no longer show mercy to the people of Israel or forgive them. ⁷ But I will show mercy to the people of Judah. I, the Lord their God, will save them, but I will not do it by war, with swords or bows and arrows, with horses and horsemen."
⁸ After Gomer had weaned her daughter, she became pregnant again and had another son. ⁹ The Lord said to Hosea, "Name him 'Not-My-People,' because the people of Israel are not my people, and I am not their God."

---

a AT JEZREEL: Here Jehu assassinated the king of Israel and all the rest of the royal family, and became the first king of a new dynasty (see 2 Kgs. 9–10).

1

Israel to Be Restored

¹⁰ The people of Israel will become like the sand of the sea, more than can be counted or measured. Now God says to them, "You are not my people," but the day is coming when he will say to them, "You are the children of the living God!" ¹¹ The people of Judah and the people of Israel will be reunited. They will choose for themselves a single leader, and once again they will grow and prosper in their land. Yes, the day of Jezreel^b

2 will be a great day! ¹ So call your fellow Israelites "God's People" and "Loved by the Lord!"

Unfaithful Gomer—Unfaithful Israel

² My children, plead with your mother—though she is no longer a wife to me, and I am no longer her husband. Plead with her to stop her adultery and prostitution. ³ If she does not, I will strip her as naked as she was on the day she was born. I will make her like a dry and barren land, and she will die of thirst. ⁴⁻⁵ I will not show mercy to her children; they are the children of a shameless prostitute. She herself said, "I will go to my lovers—they give me food and water, wool and linen, olive oil and wine."

⁶ So I am going to fence her in with thorn bushes. I will build a wall around her, so that she cannot get out. ⁷ She will try to run to her lovers, but she will not be able to get to them. She will look for them, but she will not find them. Then she will say, "I am going back to my first husband—I was better off then than I am now."

⁸ She would never acknowledge that I am the one who gave her the grain, the wine, and the olive oil. I am the one who gave her all the silver and gold that she used in the worship of Baal.^c ⁹ So at harvest time I will take back the grain and the wine I gave her, and I will take away the wool and the linen I gave her for clothing. ¹⁰ I will strip her naked in front of her lovers.

---

^b JEZREEL: This Hebrew name means "God sows" and suggests growth and prosperity.
^c BAAL: This name was the title of the Canaanite fertility god.

No one will be able to save her from my power. [11] I will put an end to all her festivities—her annual and monthly feasts, and her Sabbath celebrations—all her religious meetings. [12] I will destroy her grapevines and her fig trees, which she said her lovers gave her for serving them. I will turn her vineyards and orchards into a wilderness; wild animals will destroy them. [13] I will punish her for the times that she forgot me—when she burned incense to Baal and put on her jewelry to go chasing after her lovers. The Lord has spoken.

The Lord's Love for His People

[14] So I am going to take her into the desert again; there I will win her back with words of love. [15] I will give back to her the vineyards she had, and make Trouble Valley a door of hope. She will respond to me there as she did when she was young, when she escaped from Egypt. [16] Then once again she will call me her husband—she will no longer call me her Baal.[d] [17] I will never let her speak the name of Baal again.

[18] At that time I will make a covenant with all the wild animals and birds, so that they will not harm my people. I will remove all weapons of war from the land—all swords and bows—and let my people live in peace and security.

> [19] Israel, I will make you my wife;
> I will be true and faithful,
> I will show you constant love and
>   mercy
> and make you mine forever.
> [20] I will keep my promise and make you
>   mine,
> and you will know that I am the Lord.
> [21-22] At that time I will answer the prayers of
>   my people Jezreel.[e]
> I will make rain fall on the earth,

d BAAL: This name was the title of a Canaanite god, meaning "Lord"; it is also another word for "husband."
e JEZREEL: This word is used here as a name for the people of Israel, meaning "God sows" (see also 1.11).

and the earth will produce grain, and
   grapes, and olives.
23 I will establish my people in the land and
   make them prosper.
   I will show mercy to those who were
      called "Unloved,"
      and to those who were called "Not-
      My-People"
      I will say, "You are my people,"
      and they will answer, "You are our
      God."

Hosea and the Unfaithful Woman

3 The Lord spoke to me again. He said, "Go and
love a woman who is committing adultery with a
lover. You must love her just as I still love the people
of Israel, even though they turn to other gods and like
to take offerings of raisins to idols."*f*

2 So I paid fifteen silver coins and seven bushels of
barley to buy her. 3 I told her that she would no longer
be a prostitute, or commit adultery. I told her that she
would live with me, but for a long time would not have
intercourse with me. 4 In just this way the people of
Israel will have to live for a long time without kings or
leaders, without sacrifices or sacred stone pillars, without idols or images to use for predicting the future. 5 The
time will come when the people of Israel will once again
turn to the Lord their God, and to David their king.
Then they will fear the Lord, and will receive his good
gifts.

The Lord's Accusation against Israel

4 The Lord has an accusation to bring against the
people who live in this land. Listen, Israel, to what
he says: "There is no faithfulness or love in the land,
and the people do not acknowledge me as God. 2 They
make promises and break them; they lie, murder, steal,

---

f OFFERINGS OF RAISINS TO IDOLS: Dried grapes were used in the worship
of pagan gods, who were believed to give abundant harvests to their
worshipers.

and commit adultery. Crimes increase, and there is one murder after another. ³ And so the land will dry up, and everything that lives on it will die. All the animals and the birds—yes, even the fish—will die."

The Lord Accuses the Priests

⁴ The Lord says, "Let no one accuse the people or reprimand them—my complaint is against you priests.⁹ ⁵ Night and day you blunder on, and the prophets do no better than you. I am going to destroy Israel, your mother. ⁶ My people are doomed because they do not acknowledge me. You priests have refused to acknowledge me and have rejected my teaching, and so I reject you and your sons as my priests.

⁷ "The more of you priests there are, the more you sin against me. I will turn your honor into disgrace. ⁸ You grow rich from the sins of my people, and so you want them to sin more and more. ⁹ You will suffer the same punishment as the people! I will punish you and make you pay for the evil you do. ¹⁰ You will eat your share of the sacrifices, but still be hungry. You will worship the fertility gods, but still have no children, because you have turned away from me to follow other gods."

The Lord Condemns Pagan Worship

¹¹ The Lord says, "Wine is robbing my people of their senses! ¹² They ask for revelations from a piece of wood! A stick tells them what they want to know! They have left me. Like a woman who becomes a prostitute, they have given themselves to other gods. ¹³ At sacred places on the mountain tops they offer sacrifices, and on the hills they burn incense under tall, spreading trees, because the shade is so good!

"As a result, your daughters serve as prostitutes, and your daughters-in-law commit adultery. ¹⁴ Yet I will not punish them for this, because you yourselves go off with

---

g my complaint is against you priests; *Hebrew* your people are like those with a complaint against the priests.

"On the mountain tops they offer sacrifices." (4.13)

temple prostitutes,[h] and together with them you offer pagan sacrifices. As the proverb says, 'A people without sense will be ruined.'

[15] "Even though you people of Israel are unfaithful to me, may Judah not be guilty of the same thing. Don't worship at Gilgal or Bethel.[i] Don't make promises there in the name of the living Lord. [16] The people of Israel are as stubborn as mules. How can I feed them like lambs in a meadow? [17-18] The people of Israel are under the spell of idols. They have joined a crowd of drunkards. They keep on with their prostitution and prefer disgrace to honor. [19] They are moved by a spirit that will sweep them away like a storm, and the gods they worship will give them no help.[j]

5 "Listen to this, you priests! Pay attention, people of Israel! Listen, you that belong to the royal family! You are supposed to judge with justice—judgment will fall on you! You have become a trap at Mizpah, a net spread on Mount Tabor, [2] a deep pit at Acacia City,[k] and I will punish all of you. [3] I know what Israel is like—she cannot hide from me. She has been unfaithful, and her people are unfit to worship me."

Hosea Warns against Idolatry

[4] The evil that the people have done keeps them from returning to their God. Idolatry has a powerful hold on them, and they do not acknowledge the Lord. [5] The arrogance of the people of Israel cries out against them. Their sins make them stumble and fall, and the people of Judah fall with them. [6] They take their sheep and cattle to offer as sacrifices to the Lord, but it does them no good. They cannot find him, because he has left them. [7] They have been unfaithful to the Lord; their children do not belong to him. So now their lands will be destroyed.

---

[h] TEMPLE PROSTITUTES: These prostitutes were found in Canaanite temples, where fertility gods were worshiped. It was believed that intercourse with these women assured fertile fields and herds.
[i] BETHEL: This Hebrew name means "house of God." The Hebrew here refers to it as Bethaven, "house of evil" or "house of idolatry."
[j] *Verses 17–19 in Hebrew are unclear.*
[k] a deep pit at Acacia City; *Hebrew unclear.*

War between Judah and Israel

⁸ Blow the war trumpets in Gibeah! Sound the alarm in Ramah! Raise the war cry at Bethel!*l* Into battle, men of Benjamin! ⁹ The day of punishment is coming, and Israel will be ruined. People of Israel, this will surely happen!

¹⁰ The Lord says, "I am angry because the leaders of Judah have invaded Israel and stolen land from her. So I will pour out punishment on them like a flood. ¹¹ Israel is suffering oppression; she has lost land that was rightfully hers, because she insisted on going for help to those who had none to give.*m* ¹² I will bring destruction on Israel, and ruin on the people of Judah.

¹³ "When Israel saw how sick she was, when Judah saw her own wounds, then Israel went to Assyria to ask the great king for help, but he could not cure them or heal their wounds. ¹⁴ I will attack the people of Israel and Judah like a lion. I myself will tear them to pieces, and then leave them. When I drag them off no one will be able to save them.

¹⁵ "I will abandon my people until they have suffered enough for their sins and come looking for me. Perhaps in their suffering they will try to find me."

The People Talk of Returning to the Lord

6 The people say, "Let us return to the Lord. He has torn us, but of course he will heal us; he has wounded us, but he will bandage our wounds, won't he? ² In two or three days he will revive us, and we will live in his presence. ³ Let us try to know the Lord. He will come to us as surely as the day dawns. He will come to us as surely as the spring rains that water the earth."

The Lord's Response

⁴ The Lord says, "Israel and Judah, what am I going to do with you? Your love for me disappears as quickly as morning mist; it is like the dew, that vanishes early in the day. ⁵ That is why I have sent my prophets to you

l BETHEL: See 4.15.
m those who had none to give; *Hebrew* command.

with my message of judgment and destruction. What I want from you is plain and clear: [6] I want your constant love, not your animal sacrifices. I would rather have my people know me, than burn offerings to me.

[7] "But as soon as these people entered this promised land, they broke the covenant I had made with them. [8] Gilead is a city full of evil men and murderers. [9] The priests are like a gang of robbers who wait in ambush for a man. Even on the road to the holy place at Shechem they commit murder. And they do all this evil deliberately! [10] I have seen a horrible thing in Israel: my people have defiled themselves by worshiping idols.

[11] "And as for you, people of Judah, I have also set a time to punish you for what you are doing.

7 "Whenever I want to heal my people Israel and make them prosperous again, all I can see is their wickedness and the evil they do. They cheat each other, they break into houses and steal, they rob people in the streets. [2] It never enters their heads that I will remember all this evil; but their sins surround them and I cannot avoid seeing them."

Conspiracy in the Palace

[3] The Lord says, "People deceive the king and his officers by their evil plots. [4] They are all treacherous and disloyal. Their hatred smolders like the fire in an oven, which a baker does not stir until the dough has risen. [5] On the day of the king's celebration they made the king and his officials drunk and foolish with wine. [6] Yes, they burned[n] like an oven with their plotting. All night their anger smoldered, and in the morning it burst into flames.

[7] "In the heat of their anger they murdered their rulers. Their kings have been assassinated one after another, but no one prays to me for help."

Israel and the Nations

[8] The Lord says, "The people of Israel are no better than a half-baked loaf of bread. They rely on the nations

[n] *One ancient translation* burned; *Hebrew* drew near.

around them, [9] and do not realize that this reliance on foreigners has robbed them of their strength. Their days are numbered, but they don't even know it. [10] The arrogance of the people of Israel cries out against them. In spite of everything that has happened, they have not returned to me, the Lord their God. [11] Israel flits around like a silly pigeon; first her people call on Egypt for help, and then they run to Assyria! [12] But I will spread out a net and catch them like birds as they go by. I will punish them for the evil they have done.[o]

[13] "They are doomed! They have left me and rebelled against me. They will be destroyed. I wanted to save them, but their worship of me was false. [14] They have not prayed to me sincerely, but instead they throw themselves down and wail as the heathen do. When they pray for grain and wine, they gash themselves like pagans. What rebels they are! [15] Even though I was the one who brought them up and made them strong, they plotted against me. [16] They keep on turning away from me to gods that are powerless.[p] They are as unreliable as a crooked bow. Because their leaders talk arrogantly they will die a violent death, and the Egyptians will laugh."

The Lord Condemns Israel for Idol Worship

8 The Lord says, "Sound the alarm! Enemies are swooping down like eagles on my land! My people have broken the covenant I made with them, and rebelled against my teaching. [2] Even though they call me their God, and say that they are my people and they know me, [3] they have rejected what is good. Because of this their enemies will pursue them.

[4] "My people chose kings, but they did it on their own. They appointed leaders, but without my approval. They took their silver and gold and made idols—for their own destruction. [5] I hate the gold bull worshiped by the people of the city of Samaria. I am furious with them. How long will it be before they give up their idolatry? [6] An Israelite craftsman made the idol, and it

o the evil they have done; *Hebrew* the report to their congregation.
p gods that are powerless; *Hebrew unclear.*

is not a god at all! The gold bull worshiped in Samaria will be smashed to pieces! [7] When they sow the wind, they will reap a storm! A field of grain that doesn't ripen can never produce any bread. But even if it did, foreigners would eat it up. [8] Israel has become like any other nation, and is as useless as a broken pot. [9] Stubborn as wild donkeys, they go their own way. They have gone off to seek help from Assyria. The people of Israel have paid other nations to protect them. [10] But now I am going to gather them and punish them. Soon they will writhe in pain when the king of Assyria oppresses them.

[11] "The more altars the people of Israel build for removing sin, the more places they have for sinning! [12] I write down countless teachings for the people, but they reject them as strange and foreign. [13] They love to offer sacrifices,[q] and they love to eat the meat. But I, the Lord, am not pleased with them, and now I will remember their sin and punish them for it; I will send them back to Egypt!

[14] "The people of Israel have built palaces, but they have forgotten their own maker. The people of Judah have built fortified cities. But I will send fire that will burn down their palaces and their cities."

Hosea Announces Punishment for Israel

9 People of Israel, stop celebrating your festivals like pagans. You have turned away from your God and have been unfaithful to him. All over the land you have sold yourselves like prostitutes to Baal,[r] and loved the grain you thought he paid you with! [2] But soon you will not have enough grain and olive oil, and there will be no wine. [3] The people of Israel will not remain in the Lord's land, but will have to go back to Egypt, and have to eat forbidden food[s] in Assyria. [4] In those foreign lands they will not be able to make offerings of wine to the Lord, or bring their sacrifices to him. Their food will defile everyone who eats it, like food eaten at

q Hebrew unclear.
r BAAL: See 2.8.
s FORBIDDEN FOOD: Israelite law prohibited the eating of certain foods as ritually unclean (see Lev. 11).

funerals. Their food will be used only to satisfy their hunger; none of it will be taken as an offering to the Lord's temple. ⁵ And then, when the time comes for the appointed feasts of the Lord, what will they do? ⁶ When the disaster comes and the people are scattered, the Egyptians will gather them up—gather them for burial there at Memphis! Their treasures and the places where their homes once stood will be overgrown with weeds and thorn bushes.

⁷ The time for punishment has come, the time when people will get what they deserve. Israel will know it when that happens! "This prophet," you say, "is a fool. This inspired man is insane." You people hate me so much because your sin is so great. ⁸ God has sent me as a prophet to warn his people Israel. Yet wherever I go you try to trap me like a bird. In God's own land the people are the prophet's enemies. ⁹ They are hopelessly evil in what they do, just as they were at Gibeah.ᵗ God will remember their sins and punish them.

Israel's Sin and Its Consequences

¹⁰ The Lord says, "When I first found Israel, it was like finding grapes growing in the desert. When I first saw your ancestors, it was like seeing the first ripe figs of the season. But when they came to Mount Peor, they began to worship Baal,ᵘ and soon became as disgusting as the gods they loved. ¹¹ Israel's greatness will fly away like a bird, and there will be no more children born to them, no more women pregnant, not even any children conceived. ¹² But even if they did raise children, I would take them away, and not leave one alive. When I abandon these people, terrible things will happen to them."

¹³ Lord, I can see their children being hunted downᵛ and killed. ¹⁴ What shall I ask you to do to these people? Make their women barren! Make them unable to nurse their babies!

ᵗ AT GIBEAH: Here some Israelites of the tribe of Benjamin raped a Levite's concubine; this caused a civil war that almost wiped out the Benjaminites (see Judg. 19–21).
ᵘ BAAL: See 2.8.
ᵛ being hunted down; *Hebrew unclear.*

The Lord's Judgment on Israel

¹⁵ The Lord says, "All their evil-doing began in Gilgal. It was there that I began to hate them. And because of the evil they have done, I will drive them out of my land. I will not love them any more; all their leaders have rebelled against me. ¹⁶ The people of Israel are like a plant whose roots have dried up and which bears no fruit. They will have no children. But even if they did, I would kill the children so dear to them."

The Prophet Speaks about Israel

¹⁷ The God I serve will reject his people, because they have not listened to him. They will become wanderers **10** among the nations. ¹ The people of Israel were like a grapevine that was full of grapes. The more prosperous they were, the more altars they built. The better their land produced, the more beautiful they made the sacred stone pillars they worship. ² Their hearts are deceitful, and now they must suffer for their sins. God will break down their altars and destroy their sacred pillars.

³ These people will soon be saying, "We have no king, because we did not fear the Lord. But what could a king do for us anyway? ⁴ Nothing but talk, and make false promises and useless treaties. Justice has become injustice, growing like poisonous weeds in a plowed field."

⁵ The people who live in the city of Samaria will be afraid and will mourn the loss of the gold bull at Bethel.ʷ They and the priests who serve the idol will mourn over it. They will wail when it is stripped of its golden splendor. ⁶ The idol will be carried off to Assyria as tribute to the great king. Israel will be disgraced and put to shame because of the advice she followed. ⁷ Her king will disappear, like foam on the water. ⁸ The evil places where the people of Israel worship idols will be destroyed. Thorns and weeds will grow up over their altars. The people will call out to the mountains, "Hide us!" and to the hills, "Cover us!"

ʷ BETHEL: See 4.15.

The Lord Pronounces Judgment on Israel

[9] The Lord says, "The people of Israel have not stopped sinning against me since the time of their sin at Gibeah.[x] So war will catch up with them at Gibeah. [10] I will attack[y] this sinful people and punish them. Nations will join together against them, and they will be punished for their many sins.

[11] "Israel was once like a well-trained young cow, ready and willing to thresh grain. But I decided to put a yoke[z] on her beautiful neck, and harness her for harder work. I made Judah pull the plow and Israel pull the harrow. [12] I said, 'Plow new ground for yourselves, plant righteousness, and reap the blessings that your devotion to me will produce. It is time for you to turn to me, your Lord, and I will come and pour out blessings upon you.' [13] But instead you planted evil and reaped its harvest. You have eaten the fruit produced by your lies.

"Because you trusted in your chariots,[a] and in the large number of your soldiers, [14] war will come to your people, and all your fortresses will be destroyed. It will be like the day when King Shalman destroyed the city of Betharbel in battle, and mothers and their children were crushed to death. [15] That is what will happen to you, people of Bethel, because of the great evil that you have done. As soon as the battle begins the king of Israel will die."

God's Love for His Rebellious People

11 "When Israel was a child, I loved him,
and called him out of Egypt as my
son.
[2] But the more I[b] treated him as my son,
the more he turned away from me.[c]

---

[x] AT GIBEAH: See 9.9.
[y] *One ancient translation* I will attack; *Hebrew* In my desire.
[z] put a yoke; *Hebrew* spare.
[a] *One ancient translation* chariots; *Hebrew* way.
[b] *One ancient translation* I; *Hebrew* they.
[c] *One ancient translation* me; *Hebrew* them.

"You trusted in your chariots." (10.13)

My people sacrificed to Baal;*d*
　　they burned incense to idols.
³ Yet I was the one who taught Israel to
　　walk.
　I took my people up in my arms,*e*
　　　but they did not acknowledge that I
　　　took care of them.
⁴ I drew them to me with affection and
　　love.
　　I picked them up and held them to my
　　　cheek;
　　I bent down to them and fed them.*f*

⁵ "They refuse to return to me, and so they must
return to Egypt, and Assyria will rule them. ⁶ War will
sweep through their cities and break down the city gates.
It will destroy my people, because they do what they
themselves think best. ⁷ They have turned from me and
cannot escape the consequences. They will cry out because of the yoke that is on them, but no one will lift
it from them.*g*

⁸ "How can I give you up, Israel?
　　How could I abandon you?
　Could I destroy you as I did Admah?
　　Or treat you as I did Zeboiim?
　My heart will not let me do it!
　　My love for you is too strong.
⁹ I will not punish you in my anger;
　　I will not destroy Israel again.
　For I am God, and not man.
　　I, the Holy One, am with you.
　I will not come to you in anger.

¹⁰ "I will roar like a lion at their enemies, and my
people will follow me. They will hurry to me from the
west. ¹¹ They will come from Egypt, as swiftly as birds,
and from Assyria, like doves. I will bring them to their
homes again. I, the Lord, have spoken."

d BAAL: See 2.8.
e One ancient translation I . . . my arms; *Hebrew* He . . . his arms.
f Verse 4 in Hebrew is unclear.
g Verse 7 in Hebrew is unclear.

Israel and Judah Condemned

¹² The Lord says, "The people of Israel have surrounded me with lies and deceit. And the people of Judah are still rebelling against me, the faithful and holy God. **12** ¹ Everything that the people of Israel do from morning to night is useless and destructive. Treachery and acts of violence increase among them. They make treaties with Assyria, and do business with Egypt."

² The Lord has an accusation to bring against the people of Judah; he is also going to punish Israel for the way her people act. He will pay them back for what they have done. ³ Their ancestor Jacob struggled with his twin brother Esau while the two of them were still in their mother's womb, and when he grew up, he fought against God. ⁴ He fought against an angel, and won. Jacob wept and asked for a blessing. God came to our ancestor Jacob at Bethel, and there he spoke with him.^h ⁵ This was the Lord God Almighty—the Lord is the name by which he is to be worshiped. ⁶ So now, descendants of Jacob, trust in your God and return to him. Be loyal and just, and wait patiently for your God to act.

Further Words of Judgment

⁷ The Lord says, "The people of Israel are as dishonest as the Canaanites; they love to cheat their customers with false scales. ⁸ 'We are rich,' they say. 'We've made a fortune. And no one can accuse us of getting rich dishonestly.' ⁹ I am the Lord your God, who led you out of Egypt. I will make you live in tents again, as you did when I came to you in the desert.

¹⁰ "I spoke to the prophets and gave them many visions. Through the prophets I gave my people warnings. ¹¹ Idols are worshiped in Gilead, and those who worship them will die. Bulls are sacrificed in Gilgal, and so the altars will become piles of stone in the open fields."

¹² Our ancestor Jacob had to flee to the land of Aram, where, in order to get a wife, he worked for another

^h *Some ancient translations* him; *Hebrew* us.

man and took care of his sheep. [13] The Lord sent a
prophet to rescue the people of Israel from slavery in
Egypt, and to take care of them. [14] The people of Israel
have made the Lord bitterly angry; they deserve death
for their crimes. God will punish them for the disgrace
they have brought on him.

Final Judgment on Israel

13 In the past, when the tribe of Ephraim spoke,
others were afraid. The other tribes of Israel
looked up to Ephraim. But the people sinned by worshiping Baal,[i] and for this they will die. [2] They still
keep on sinning, and make metal images to worship.
They make idols out of their silver, designed by human
minds, made by human hands. And then they say,
"Offer sacrifices to them!" How can men kiss those
idols—idols in the shape of bulls![j] [3] And so these people
will disappear like morning mist, like the dew that
vanishes early in the day. They will be like straw which
the wind blows from the threshing floor, like smoke
from a chimney.

[4] The Lord says, "I am the Lord your God, who led
you out of Egypt. You have no God but me. I alone
am your savior. [5] I took care of you in a dry, desert
land. [6] But when you entered the good land, you became
full and satisfied, and then you became proud and forgot
me. [7] So I will attack you like a lion. Like a leopard I
will lie in wait along your path. [8] I will attack you like
a bear that has lost her cubs, and tear you open. Like
a lion I will devour you on the spot, and tear you to
pieces like a wild animal.

[9] "I will destroy you, people of Israel! Then who
can help you?[k] [10] You asked for a king and for leaders.
But how can they save the nation?[l] [11] In my anger I
have given you kings, and in my fury I have taken them
away.

---

[i] BAAL: See 2.8.
[j] And then they . . . bulls; *Hebrew unclear.*
[k] *One ancient translation* who can help you?; *Hebrew* in me is your
help.
[l] *Verse 10 in Hebrew is unclear.*

12 "Israel's sin and guilt are on record, and the records are safely stored away. 13 Israel has a chance to live, but is too foolish to take it—like a child about to be born, who will not come out of the womb. 14 I will not save this people from the world of the dead,*m* or rescue them from the power of death. Bring on*n* your plagues, death! Bring on*n* your destruction, world of the dead! I will no longer have pity for this people. 15 Even though Israel flourishes like weeds,*o* I will send a hot east wind from the desert, and it will dry up their springs and wells. It will take away everything of value. 16 Samaria must be punished for rebelling against God. Her people will die in war; babies will be dashed to the ground, and pregnant women will be ripped open."

Hosea's Plea to Israel

14 Return to the Lord your God, people of Israel. Your sin has made you stumble and fall. 2 Return to the Lord, and let this prayer be your offering to him: "Forgive all our sins, and accept our prayer, and we will praise you as we have promised. 3 Assyria can never save us, and war chariots cannot protect us. We will never again say to our idols, 'You are our God.' We confess, O Lord, that you show mercy to those who have no one else to turn to."

The Lord Promises New Life for Israel

4 I will bring my people back to me.
   I will love them with all my heart;
      I am no longer angry with them.
5 I will be to the people of Israel
   like rain in a dry land.
   They will blossom like flowers;
      they will be firmly rooted
      like the trees of Lebanon.
6 They will be alive with new growth,
      and beautiful, like olive trees.

---

m WORLD OF THE DEAD: It was thought that the dead continued to exist in a dark world under the ground.
n Bring on; *Hebrew* I will be.
o like weeds; *Hebrew* among brothers.

"They will be firmly rooted like the trees of Lebanon." (14.5)

They will be fragrant,
   like the cedars of Lebanon.
⁷ Once again they will live under my
   protection.
They will flourish like a garden*p*
   and be fruitful like a vineyard.
   They will be as famous as the wine of
   Lebanon.
⁸ The people of Israel*q* will have nothing
   more to do with idols,
   I will answer their prayers and take
   care of them.
I will shelter them like an evergreen tree;
   I am the source of all their blessings.

Conclusion

⁹ May those who are wise understand what is written
here and take it to heart. The Lord's ways are right,
and righteous men live by following them, but sinners
stumble and fall because they ignore them.

p flourish like a garden; *Hebrew* grow grain.
q One ancient translation The people of Israel; *Hebrew* Israel, I.

AMOS

1 These are the words of Amos, a shepherd from the village of Tekoa. God revealed these things to him about Israel two years before the earthquake, when Uzziah was king of Judah, and Jeroboam son of Joash was king of Israel.

² Amos said,

> "The Lord roars from Zion;
> his voice thunders from Jerusalem.
> The pastures dry up,
> and the grass on Mount Carmel turns
> brown."

God's Judgment on Israel's Neighbors

Syria

³ The Lord says, "The people of Damascus have sinned again and again, and I will surely punish them. They have treated the people of Gilead with savage cruelty. ⁴ So I will throw fire down on the royal palace of Syria, and burn down the fortresses of King Benhadad. ⁵ I will smash the city gates of Damascus and remove the rulers of Betheden and of Aven Valley. The people of Syria will be taken away as prisoners to the land of Kir."

Philistia

⁶ The Lord says, "The people of Gaza have sinned again and again, and I will surely punish them. They carried off a whole nation and sold them as slaves to the people of Edom. ⁷ So I will throw fire down on the city walls of Gaza and burn down its fortresses. ⁸ I will remove the rulers of the cities of Ashdod and Ashkelon. I will punish the city of Ekron, and all the Philistines who are left will die."

"I will . . . burn down the fortresses of King Benhadad." (1.4)

Tyre

⁹ The Lord says, "The people of Tyre have sinned again and again, and I will surely punish them. They carried off a whole nation into exile in the land of Edom. They did not keep the treaty of friendship they had made. ¹⁰ So I will throw fire down on the city walls of Tyre and burn down its fortresses."

Edom

¹¹ The Lord says, "The people of Edom have sinned again and again, and I will surely punish them. They hunted down their brothers, the Israelites, and showed them no mercy. Their anger had no limits, and they never let it die. ¹² So I will throw fire down on the city of Teman, and burn down the fortresses of Bozrah."

Ammon

¹³ The Lord says, "The people of Ammon have sinned again and again, and I will surely punish them. In their wars for more territory they even ripped open pregnant women in Gilead. ¹⁴ So I will throw fire down on the city walls of Rabbah and burn down its fortresses. Then there will be shouts on the day of battle, and the fighting will rage like a storm. ¹⁵ Their king and his officers will go into exile."

Moab

2 The Lord says, "The people of Moab have sinned again and again, and I will surely punish them. They dishonored the bones of the king of Edom by burning them to ashes. ² I will throw fire down on the land of Moab and burn down the fortresses of Kerioth. The people of Moab will die in the noise of battle, while soldiers are shouting and trumpets are sounding. ³ I will kill the ruler of Moab and all the leaders of the land."

Judah

⁴ The Lord says, "The people of Judah have sinned again and again, and I will surely punish them. They

have despised my teachings and have not kept my commands. They have been led astray by the same false gods that their ancestors served. ⁵ So I will throw fire down on Judah and burn down the fortresses of Jerusalem."

God's Judgment on Israel

⁶ The Lord says, "The people of Israel have sinned again and again, and I will surely punish them. They sell into slavery honest men who cannot pay their debts, poor men who cannot repay even the price of a pair of sandals. ⁷ They trample[a] down the weak and helpless and push the poor out of the way. Men young and old go to the temple prostitutes,[b] and so profane my holy name. ⁸ At every place of worship men sleep on clothing they have taken from the poor as security for debts. In the temple of their God they drink wine which they have taken from those who owe them money.

⁹ "And yet, my people, it was for your sake that I totally destroyed the Amorites, men who were as tall as cedar trees and as strong as oaks. ¹⁰ I brought you out of Egypt, led you through the desert for forty years, and gave you the land of the Amorites to be your own. ¹¹ I chose some of your sons to be prophets, and some of your young men to be Nazirites.[c] Isn't this true, people of Israel? I, the Lord, have spoken. ¹² But you made the Nazirites drink wine, and ordered the prophets not to speak my message. ¹³ And now I will crush you to the ground, and you will groan like a cart loaded with grain. ¹⁴ Not even fast runners will escape; strong men will lose their strength, and soldiers will not be able to save their own lives. ¹⁵ Bowmen will not stand their ground, fast runners will not get away, and men on horses will not escape with their lives. ¹⁶ On that day even the bravest soldiers will drop their weapons and run." The Lord has spoken.

a trample; *Hebrew unclear.*
b TEMPLE PROSTITUTES: These prostitutes were found in Canaanite temples, where fertility gods were worshiped. It was believed that intercourse with these women assured fertile fields and herds.
c NAZIRITES: These were people who showed their devotion to God by taking vows not to use alcohol, cut their hair, or touch dead bodies.

"You will groan like a cart loaded with grain." (2.13)

3 People of Israel, listen to this message which the Lord has spoken about you, the whole nation that he brought out of Egypt: [2] "Of all the nations on earth you are the only one I have known and cared for. That is why I will punish you for all your sins."

The Prophet's Task

[3] Do two men start traveling together without arranging to meet?

[4] Does a lion roar in the forest unless he has found a victim?

Does a young lion growl in his den unless he has caught something?

[5] Does a bird get caught in a trap if the trap has not been baited?

Does a trap spring unless something sets it off?

[6] Does the war trumpet sound in a city without making the people afraid?

Does disaster strike a city unless the Lord sends it?

[7] Surely the Lord never does anything without revealing his plan to his servants, the prophets.

[8] When a lion roars, who can keep from being afraid?

When the Lord speaks, who can keep from proclaiming his message?

The Doom of Samaria

[9] Announce to those who live in the palaces of Egypt and Ashdod: "Gather together in the city of Samaria and see the great disorder, and the crimes being committed there."

[10] The Lord says, "These people fill their mansions with things taken by crime and violence. They don't even know how to be honest. [11] And so an enemy will surround their land, destroy their defenses, and plunder their mansions."

[12] The Lord says, "As a shepherd recovers only two legs and an ear of a sheep that a lion has eaten, so only a few of Samaria's luxury-loving[d] people will survive.

d luxury-loving; *Hebrew unclear.*

¹³ Listen now, and warn the descendants of Jacob," says the Lord God Almighty. ¹⁴ "On the day when I punish the people of Israel for their sins I will destroy the altars of Bethel. The corners of every altar will be broken off and will fall to the ground. ¹⁵ I will destroy winter houses and summer houses. The houses decorated with ivory will fall in ruins, and every large house will be destroyed."

4 Listen to this, you women of Samaria, who grow fat like well-fed cows, who mistreat the weak, oppress the poor, and order your husbands to bring you something to drink! ² As the Lord is holy, he has promised, "The days will come when they will drag you away with hooks; every one of you will be like a fish on a hook. ³ You will be dragged to the nearest break in the wall and thrown out."ᵉ

Israel's Failure to Learn

⁴ The Lord says, "People of Israel, go to the holy place in Bethel—and sin! Go to Gilgal and sin with all your might! Bring animals to be sacrificed morning after morning, and bring your tithes every third day. ⁵ Go on and offer your bread in thanksgiving to God, and brag about the extra offerings you bring! This is the kind of thing you love to do.

⁶ "I was the one who brought famine to all your cities, so that you had no food. Yet you did not come back to me. ⁷ I kept it from raining when your crops needed it most. I sent rain on one city, but not on another. One field got rain, but another one dried up. ⁸ Weak with thirst, the people of two or three cities went to a neighboring city to find water, but there was not enough to drink. Still you did not come back to me.

⁹ "I sent a scorching wind to dry up your crops. The locusts ate up all your gardens and vineyards, your fig trees and olive trees. Still you did not come back to me.

ᵉ *The Hebrew has an additional word, the meaning of which is unclear.*

¹⁰ "I sent a plague on you like the one I sent on Egypt. I killed your young men in battle, and took your horses away. I filled your nostrils with the stink of dead bodies in your camps. Still you did not come back to me.

¹¹ "I destroyed some of you as I destroyed Sodom and Gomorrah. Those of you who survived were like a burning stick saved from a fire. Still you did not come back to me," says the Lord. ¹² "So then, people of Israel, I am going to punish you. And because I am going to do this, get ready to face God's judgment!"

¹³ God is the one who made the mountains
and created the winds.
He makes his thoughts known to man;
he changes day into night.
He rules over all the earth.
This is his name: the Lord God
Almighty!

A Call to Repentance

5 Listen, people of Israel, to this funeral song which I sing over you:

² Israel has fallen,
never to rise again.
She lies on the ground,
and no one helps her up.

³ The Lord says, "A city in Israel sends out a thousand soldiers, but only a hundred return; another city sends out a hundred, but only ten come back."

⁴ The Lord says to the people of Israel, "Come to me, and you will live. ⁵ Do not go to Beersheba to worship. Do not try to find me at Bethel—Bethel will come to nothing. Do not go to Gilgal—her people are doomed to exile." ⁶ Go to the Lord, and you will live. If you do not, he will sweep down like fire on the people of Israel. The fire will burn up the people of Bethel; no one can put it out. ⁷ You are doomed, you that twist justice and cheat people out of their rights!

⁸ The Lord made the stars,
    the Pleiades and Orion.
He turns darkness to daylight,
    and day into night.
He calls the waters of the sea
    and pours them out on the earth.
His name is the Lord.
⁹ He brings destruction on forts and strong-
        holds.

¹⁰ You people hate anyone who challenges injustice and who speaks the whole truth in court. ¹¹ You have oppressed the poor and robbed them of their grain. And so you will not live in the fine stone houses you build, or drink wine from the beautiful vineyards you plant. ¹² I know how terrible your sins are and how many crimes you have committed. You persecute good men, take bribes, and keep the poor from getting justice in the courts. ¹³ Keeping quiet in such evil times is the smart thing to do!

¹⁴ Work for what is right, not for what is evil, so that you may live. Then the Lord God Almighty really will be with you, as you claim he is. ¹⁵ Hate evil, love good, see that justice prevails in the courts. Perhaps the Lord will be merciful to the people of this nation who are still left alive.

¹⁶ And so the Lord God Almighty says, "There will be wailing and cries of sorrow in the city streets. Farmers will be called to mourn the dead along with those who are paid to mourn. ¹⁷ There will be wailing in all the vineyards. All this will take place because I am coming to punish you." The Lord has spoken.

¹⁸ How terrible it will be for you who long for the day of the Lord! What good will that day do you? It will be a day of darkness, and not of light. ¹⁹ It will be like a man who runs from a lion and meets a bear! Or like a man who comes home and puts his hand on the wall—only to be bitten by a snake! ²⁰ The day of the Lord will bring darkness, and not light; it will be a day of gloom, without any brightness.

²¹ The Lord says, "I hate your religious feasts, I cannot stand them! ²² When you bring me burnt offerings and grain offerings, I will not accept them, nor will I accept the animals you have fattened to bring me as offerings. ²³ Stop your noisy songs; I do not want to listen to your harps. ²⁴ Let justice flow like a stream, and righteousness like a river that never goes dry.

²⁵ "People of Israel, during those forty years in the desert you did not bring me sacrifices and offerings. ²⁶ So now you will have to carry the images of your star gods, Sakkuth and Kaiwan, which you made for yourselves, ²⁷ and I will take you into exile in a land beyond Damascus," says the Lord, whose name is Almighty God.

The Destruction of Israel

6 How terrible it will be for you that have such an easy life in Zion, and for you that feel safe in Samaria—you great men of this great nation Israel, you to whom the people go for help! ² Go and look at the city of Calneh. Then go on to the great city of Hamath, and on down to the Philistine city of Gath. Were they any better than the kingdoms of Judah and Israel? Was their territory larger than yours? ³ You refuse to admit that a day of disaster is coming, but your actions encourage violence. ⁴ How terrible it will be for you that lie on luxurious beds, and stretch out on your couches, and feast on veal and lamb! ⁵ You like to compose songs, as David did, and play them on harps. ⁶ You drink wine by the bowlful, and use the finest perfumes, but you do not mourn over the ruin of Israel. ⁷ So you will be the first to go into exile. Your feasts and banquets will come to an end.

⁸ The Lord God Almighty has given this solemn warning: "I hate the pride of the people of Israel, and their luxurious mansions. I will give their capital city and everything in it to the enemy."

⁹ If there are ten men left in a family, they will all die. ¹⁰ Then when a dead man's relative comes to take out the body and burn it, he will call to whoever is hiding in the house, "Is there anyone else there?"

A voice answers, "No!"

So he will say, "Be quiet! We must be careful not even to mention the Lord's name."

¹¹ When the Lord gives the command, houses large and small will be smashed to pieces. ¹² Do horses run on cliffs? Do men plow the sea with oxen? Yet you have turned justice into poison, and made right come out as wrong. ¹³ You brag about capturing the town of Lodebar.*f* You say, "We were strong enough to take Karnaim."*g*

¹⁴ The Lord God Almighty himself answers, "People of Israel, I am going to send a foreign army to occupy your country. It will oppress you from Hamath Pass in the north to the Dead Sea in the south."

A Vision of Locusts

7 I had a vision from the Lord. In it I saw him create a swarm of locusts just after the king's share of the hay had been cut, and the grass was starting to grow again. ² In my vision I saw the locusts eat up every green thing in the land, and then I said, "Forgive your people, Lord! How can they survive? They are so small and weak!"

³ The Lord changed his mind and said, "What you saw will not take place."

A Vision of Fire

⁴ I had a vision from the Lord. In it I saw him preparing to punish his people with fire. The fire burned up the great ocean under the earth,*h* and started to burn up the land. ⁵ Then I said, "Stop, Lord! How can your people survive? They are so small and weak!"

⁶ The Lord changed his mind and said, "This will not take place either."

---

f LODEBAR: This name sounds like the Hebrew for "nothing."
g KARNAIM: This Hebrew name means "horns," a symbol of strength.
h THE GREAT OCEAN UNDER THE EARTH: The ancient Hebrews believed that under the earth there was a great body of water which sometimes broke through the earth's surface (see Gen. 7.11).

A Vision of a Plumb Line

7 I had a vision from the Lord. In it I saw him standing beside a wall that had been built with the use of a plumb line, and there was a plumb line in his hand. 8 He asked me, "Amos, what do you see?"

"A plumb line," I answered.

Then he said, "I am using it to show that my people are like a wall that is out of line. I will not change my mind again about punishing them. 9 The places where Isaac's descendants worship will be destroyed. The holy places of Israel will be left in ruins. I will bring the dynasty of King Jeroboam to an end."

Amos and Amaziah

10 Amaziah, the priest of Bethel, then sent a report to King Jeroboam of Israel, "Amos is plotting against you among the people. His speeches will destroy the country. 11 This is what he says, 'Jeroboam will die in battle, and the people of Israel will be taken away from their land into exile.'"

12 Amaziah then said to Amos, "That's enough, prophet! Go on back to Judah and do your preaching there. Let *them* pay you for it. 13 Don't prophesy here at Bethel any more. This is the king's place of worship, the national temple."

14 Amos answered, "I am not the kind of prophet who prophesies for pay. I am a herdsman, and I take care of fig trees. 15 But the Lord took me from my work as a shepherd and ordered me to go and prophesy to his people Israel. 16 So now listen to what the Lord says. You tell me to stop prophesying, to stop raving against the people of Israel. 17 Because you say that, Amaziah, the Lord says to you, 'Your wife will become a prostitute in the city, and your children will be killed in war. Your land will be divided up and given to others, and you yourself will die in a heathen country. The people of Israel will be taken away from their own land into exile.'"

"There was a plumb line in his hand." (7.7)

"Go on back to Judah and do your preaching there." (7.12)

A Vision of a Basket of Fruit

8 I had a vision from the Lord. In it I saw a basket of fruit. [2] The Lord asked, "Amos, what do you see?"

"A basket of fruit," I answered.

The Lord said to me, "The end[i] has come for my people Israel. I will not change my mind again about punishing them. [3] On that day the songs in the palace will become cries of mourning. There will be dead bodies everywhere. Not a sound will be heard."

Israel's Doom

[4] Listen to this, you that trample on the needy, and try to destroy the poor of the country. [5] You say to yourselves, "We can hardly wait for the holy days to be over so that we can sell our grain. When will the Sabbath end, so that we can start selling again? Then we can overcharge, use false measures, and fix the scales to cheat our customers. [6] We can sell worthless wheat at a high price. We'll find a poor man who can't pay his debts, not even the price of a pair of sandals, and buy him as a slave."

[7] The Lord, the God of Israel, has sworn, "I will never forget their evil deeds. [8] And so the earth will quake, and everyone in the land will be in distress. The whole country will be shaken; it will rise and fall like the Nile River. [9] On that day I will make the sun go down at noon, and the earth grow dark in daytime. I, the Lord, have spoken. [10] I will turn your festivals into funerals, and change your glad songs to cries of grief. I will make you shave your heads and wear sackcloth. You will be like parents mourning for their only son. That day will be bitter to the end.

[11] "The time is coming when I will send famine on the land. People will be hungry, but not for bread; they will be thirsty, but not for water. They will be hungry for a message from the Lord. I, the Lord, have spoken. [12] People will wander from north to south and from east to west. They will look everywhere for a message from

[i] END: The Hebrew words for "end" and "fruit" are similar.

"We'll find a poor man . . . and buy him as a slave." (8.6)

the Lord, but they will not find it. ¹³ On that day even pretty girls and strong young men will collapse from thirst. ¹⁴ Those who swear by the idols of Samaria, who say, 'By the god of Dan,' or, 'By the god of Beersheba' —these people will fall and not rise again."

The Lord's Judgments

9 I saw the Lord standing by the altar. He gave the command: "Strike the top of the temple columns so that the whole porch will shake. Break them off and let them fall on the heads of the people. I will kill the rest of the people in war. No one will get away; not one will escape. ² Even if they dig their way down to the world of the dead,^j I will catch them. Even if they climb up to heaven, I will bring them down. ³ If they hide on the top of Mount Carmel, I will search for them and catch them. If they hide from me at the bottom of the sea, I will command the sea monster^k to swallow them. ⁴ If they are taken away into captivity by their enemies, I will order them to be put to death. I am determined to destroy them, and not help them."

> ⁵ The Lord God Almighty touches the earth,
> and it quakes;
> all who live there mourn.
> The whole world rises and falls like the Nile River.
> ⁶ The Lord builds his rooms in the heavens,
> and puts the dome of the sky over the earth.
> He calls for the waters of the sea
> and pours them out on the earth.
> His name is the Lord!

⁷ The Lord says, "People of Israel, I think as much of the Ethiopians as I do of you. I brought the Philis-

---

^j WORLD OF THE DEAD: It was thought that the dead continued to exist in a dark world under the ground.
^k SEA MONSTER: It was believed that the sea was inhabited by a great monster. This creature, like all others, was under God's control.

tines from Crete, and the Syrians from Kir, just as I brought you from Egypt. [8] I am watching this sinful kingdom of Israel, and I will destroy it from the face of the earth. But I will not destroy all the descendants of Jacob.

[9] "I will give the command and shake the people of Israel like grain in a sieve. I will shake them among the nations to remove all who are worthless. [10] The sinners among my people will be killed in war—all those who say, 'God will not let any harm come near us.' "

The Future Restoration of Israel

[11] The Lord says, "A day is coming when I will restore the kingdom of David, which is like a house fallen into ruins. I will repair its walls, and restore it. I will rebuild it and make it as it was long ago. [12] And so the people of Israel will conquer what is left of the land of Edom and all the nations that were once mine," says the Lord, who will cause this to happen.

[13] "The days are coming," says the Lord,
> "when grain will grow faster than it
> can be harvested,
> and grapes will grow faster than the
> wine can be made.
The mountains will drip with sweet wine,
> and the hills will flow with it.
[14] I will bring my people back to their land.
> They will rebuild their ruined cities
> and live there;
> they will plant vineyards and drink the
> wine;
> they will plant gardens and eat what
> they grow.
[15] I will plant my people on the land I gave
> them,
> and they will not be pulled up again."
The Lord your God has spoken.

"The mountains will drip with sweet wine." (9.13)

MICAH

1 This is the message which the Lord gave to Micah of the town of Moresheth, during the time that Jotham, Ahaz, and Hezekiah were kings of Judah. The Lord revealed these things to Micah about Samaria and Jerusalem.

A Lament for Samaria and Jerusalem

2 Hear this, all you nations;
  listen to this, all who live on earth!
The Lord God will testify against you.
  Listen! He speaks from his heavenly
    temple.
3 The Lord is coming from his holy place;
  he will come down and walk on the
    tops of the mountains.
4 Then the mountains will melt under him
  like wax in a fire;
they will pour down into the valleys
  like water pouring down a hill.

5 All this will happen because the people of Israel have sinned and rebelled against God. Who is to blame for Israel's rebellion? Samaria, the capital city itself! Who is guilty of idolatry in Judah? Jerusalem itself! 6 So the Lord says, "I will make Samaria a pile of ruins in the open country, a place for planting grapevines. I will pour the rubble of the city down into the valley, and lay bare the city's foundations. 7 All its precious idols will be smashed to pieces and destroyed by fire. The people were unfaithful to God when they made these idols, and now they will get what their unfaithfulness deserves."

"I will make Samaria a pile of ruins in the open country." (1.6)

8 Then Micah said, "Because of this I will mourn and lament. I will walk around barefoot and naked, to show my sorrow. I will howl like a jackal and wail like an ostrich. 9 Samaria's wounds cannot be healed, and Judah is about to suffer in the same way; destruction has reached the gates of Jerusalem itself, where my people live."

The Enemy Approaches Jerusalem

10 Don't tell our enemies in Gath about our defeat; don't let them see you weeping. Show your despair, people of Beth Leaphrah!a 11 You people of Shaphir, go into exile, naked and ashamed. Those who live in Zaanan will never get out alive. When you hear the people of Bethezel mourn, you will know there is no refuge there. 12 The people of Maroth twist in pain; they long for relief, because the Lord has brought disaster close to Jerusalem. 13 You that live in Lachish, hitch the horses to the chariots. You imitated the sins of Israel, and so caused Jerusalem to sin. 14 And now, people of Judah, say good-bye to the town of Moresheth Gath. The kings of Israel will get no help from the town of Achzib.

15 People of Mareshah, the Lord will hand you over to an enemy, who is going to take your town. The king of Israel will go and hide in the cave at Adullam. 16 People of Judah, cut off your hair in mourning for the children you love. Make yourselves as bald as vultures, because your children will be taken away from you into exile.

The Fate of Those Who Oppress the Poor

2 How terrible it will be for those who lie in bed and plan evil! When morning comes, as soon as they have the chance, they do the evil they planned. 2 When they want fields, they take them. When they want houses, they take them. No man's family or property is safe.

a BETH LEAPHRAH: As an invading army approaches Jerusalem, the prophet speaks of the outlying towns that are attacked (vv. 10–14).

"Its precious idols will be smashed to pieces." (1.7)

³ And so the Lord says, "I am planning to bring disaster on you, and you will not be able to escape it. You are going to find yourselves in trouble, and then you will not walk so proudly any more. ⁴ When that time comes, people will use your story as an example of disaster, and sing this despairing song about your experience:

> We are completely ruined!
> The Lord has taken our land away.
> He has given it to those who took us
>   captive."*b*

⁵ So then, when the time comes that the land is given back to the Lord's people, there will be no share for any of you.

⁶ The people preach at me, "Don't preach at us. Don't preach about all that. God is not going to disgrace us. ⁷ Do you think the people of Israel are under a curse?*c* Has the Lord lost his patience? Would he really do such things? Doesn't he*d* speak kindly to those who do right?"

⁸ The Lord replies, "You attack my people like enemies. Men return from battle, thinking they are safe at home, but there you are, waiting to steal the coats off their backs.*e* ⁹ You drive the women of my people out of the homes they love, and you have robbed their children forever of my blessings. ¹⁰ Get up and go; there is no safety here any more. Your sins have doomed this place to destruction.

¹¹ "These people want the kind of prophet who goes around full of lies and deceit and says, 'I prophesy that wine and liquor will flow for you.'

¹² "But I will gather you together, all you people of Israel that are left. I will bring you together like sheep returning to the fold. Like a pasture full of sheep, once again your land will be filled with many people."

¹³ God will open the way for them and lead them out of exile. They will break out of the city gates and go free. Their king, the Lord himself, will lead them out.

---

b those who took us captive; *Hebrew* rebels.
c under a curse; *Hebrew unclear.*
d Doesn't he; *Hebrew* Don't I.
e Verse 8 in Hebrew is unclear.

Micah Denounces Israel's Leaders

3 Listen, you rulers of Israel! You are supposed to be concerned about justice, ² but you hate what is good and love what is evil. You skin my people alive and tear the flesh off their bones. ³ You eat my people up. You strip off their skin, break their bones, and chop them up like meat for the pot. ⁴ The time is coming when you will cry out to the Lord, but he will not answer you. He will not listen to your prayers, because you have done evil.

⁵ My people are deceived by prophets who promise peace to those who pay them, but threaten war for those who don't. To these prophets the Lord says, ⁶ "Prophets, your day is almost over; the sun is going down on you. Because you mislead my people, you will have no more prophetic visions, and you will not be able to predict anything." ⁷ Those who predict the future will be disgraced by their failure. They will all be humiliated because God does not answer them.

⁸ But as for me, the Lord's spirit fills me with power, judgment, and courage to tell the people of Israel what their sins are. ⁹ Listen to me, you rulers of Israel, you that hate justice and turn right into wrong. ¹⁰ You are building God's city, Jerusalem, on a foundation of murder and injustice. ¹¹ The city's rulers govern for bribes, the priests interpret the Law for pay, the prophets give their revelations for money—and they all claim the Lord is with them. "No harm will come to us," they say. "The Lord is with us."

¹² And so, because of you, Zion will be plowed like a field, Jerusalem will become a pile of ruins, and the temple hill will become a forest.

The Lord's Universal Reign of Peace

4 In days to come,
the mountain where the Temple stands
will be the highest one of all.
Many nations will come streaming to it,
² and their people will say,
"Let us go up the hill of the Lord,
to the Temple of Israel's God.

We will learn what he wants us to do;
    we will walk in the paths he has
      chosen."

The Lord's teaching comes from
    Jerusalem;
    from Zion he speaks to his people.
³ He will settle disputes among the nations,
    among great powers near and far.
They will hammer their swords into
    plows,
    and their spears into pruning knives.
Nations will never again go to war,
    never prepare for war again.
⁴ Everyone will live in peace
    among his own vineyards and fig trees,
    and no one will make him afraid.
The Lord Almighty has promised this.

⁵ Each nation worships and obeys its own god, but we will worship and obey the Lord, our God, forever and ever.

Israel Will Return from Exile

⁶ "The time is coming," says the Lord, "when I will gather together the people I punished, those who have suffered in exile. ⁷ They are crippled and far from home, but I will make a new beginning with them, and they will become a great nation. I will rule over them on Mount Zion from that time on and forever."

⁸ And you, Jerusalem, where God watches over his people, you will once again be the capital of the kingdom that was yours. ⁹ Why do you cry out so loudly? Why are you suffering like a woman in labor? Is it because you have no king, and your counselors are dead? ¹⁰ Twist and groan,ᶠ people of Jerusalem, like a woman giving birth, for now you will have to leave the city and live in the open country. You will have to go to Babylon. But there you will be rescued, and the Lord will save you from your enemies.

_f_ groan; _Hebrew_ bring forth.

"They will hammer their swords into plows." (4.3)

¹¹ Many nations have gathered to attack you. They say, "Jerusalem must be destroyed! We will see this city in ruins!" ¹² But these nations do not know what is in the Lord's mind. They do not know that he has gathered them together to punish them, in the same way that grain is brought in to be threshed.

¹³ The Lord says, "People of Jerusalem, go and punish your enemies! I will make you as strong as a bull with iron horns and bronze hoofs. You will crush many nations, and the wealth they got by violence will belong to me, the Lord of the whole world."

5 People of Jerusalem, gather your forces!ᵍ We are besieged! They are attacking the leader of Israel!

God Promises a Ruler from Bethlehem

² The Lord says, "Bethlehem Ephrathah, you are one of the smallest towns in Judah, but out of you I will bring a ruler for Israel, whose family line goes back to ancient times."

³ So the Lord will abandon his people to their enemies until the one who is to give birth has her son. Then his fellow countrymen who are in exile will be reunited with their own people. ⁴ When he comes he will rule his people with the strength that comes from the Lord, and with the majesty of the Lord God himself. His people will live in safety, because men all over the earth will acknowledge his greatness, ⁵ and he will bring peace.

Deliverance and Punishment

When the Assyrians invade our country and break through our defenses, we will send our strongest leaders to fight them, ⁶ and they will conquer the land of Assyria by force of arms. Theyʰ will save us from the Assyrians when they invade our territory.

⁷ The people of Israel who survive will be like refreshing dew sent by the Lord for many nations, like showers on growing plants. They will depend on God, not man.

ᵍ People . . . forces; *Hebrew unclear.*
ʰ They; *Hebrew He.*

[8] Some of the people of Israel will be left among the nations like a lion hunting for food in a forest or a pasture. He gets in among the sheep, pounces on them and tears them to pieces—and there is no hope of rescue. [9] Israel will conquer her enemies and destroy them all.

[10] The Lord says, "At that time I will take away your horses and destroy your chariots. [11] I will destroy the cities in your land and tear down all your defenses. [12] I will destroy the magic charms you use, and not leave you any fortunetellers. [13] I will destroy the idols and the sacred stone pillars that you worship. You will no longer worship the things that you have made. [14] I will pull down the sacred poles in your country, and destroy your cities. [15] And in my great anger I will take revenge on all nations that have not obeyed me."

The Lord's Case against Israel

6 Listen to the Lord's case against Israel. Arise, O Lord, and present your case; let the mountains and the hills hear what you say.

[2] You mountains, you everlasting foundations of the earth, listen to the Lord's case! The Lord has a case against his people. He is going to bring an accusation against Israel.

[3] The Lord says, "My people, what have I done to you? How have I been a burden to you? Answer me. [4] I brought you out of Egypt. I rescued you from slavery. I sent Moses, Aaron, and Miriam to lead you. [5] My people, remember what King Balak of Moab planned to do to you, and how Balaam son of Beor answered him. Remember the things that happened on the way from the camp at Acacia to Gilgal. Remember these things and you will realize what I did in order to save you."

What the Lord Requires

[6] What shall I bring to the Lord, the God of heaven, when I come to worship him? Shall I bring the best calves to burn as offerings to him? [7] Will the Lord be

"He . . . pounces on them and tears them to pieces." (5.8)

pleased if I bring him thousands of sheep, or endless
streams of olive oil? Shall I offer him my firstborn child
to pay for my sins? [8] No, the Lord has told us what is
good. What he requires of us is this: to do what is just,
show constant love, and humbly obey our God.

[9] It is wise to fear the Lord. He calls to the city,
"Listen, you people who assemble in the city.[i] [10] In the
houses of evil men are treasures which they got dis-
honestly. They use false measures, a thing that I hate.[j]
[11] How can I forgive men who use false scales and
weights? [12] The city's rich men exploit the poor, and
her people are liars. [13] So now I have already begun[k]
your ruin and destruction, because of your sins. [14] You
will eat, but not be satisfied. You will still be hungry.
When you carry things off to save them, you will not
succeed. Anything you do save, I will destroy in war.
[15] You will sow grain, but not harvest the crop. You
will press oil from olives, but never get to use it. You
will make wine, but never get to drink it. [16] You have followed the evil practices of King Omri and of his son,
King Ahab. You have continued their policies, and so
I will bring you to ruin, and everyone will despise you.
People[l] everywhere will treat you with contempt."

Israel's Moral Corruption

7 It's hopeless! I am like a hungry man who finds
no fruit left on the trees and no grapes on the
vines. All the grapes, all the tasty figs have been picked.
[2] There is not an honest man left in the land, no one
loyal to God. Everyone is waiting for a chance to commit murder. Everyone hunts down his fellow country-
man. [3] They are all experts at doing evil. Officials and
judges ask for bribes. The influential man tells them
what he wants, and so they scheme together.[m] [4] Even
the best and most honest of them are as worthless as
weeds.

---

[i] who assemble in the city; *Hebrew* and who appointed it. **Yet.**
[j] *Verse 10 in Hebrew is unclear.*
[k] *Some ancient translations* begun; *Hebrew* made sick.
[l] *One ancient translation* People; *Hebrew* My people.
[m] and so they scheme together; *Hebrew unclear.*

"The influential man tells them what he wants, and so they scheme together." (7.3)

The day has come when God will punish the people, as he warned them through the prophet. Now they are in confusion. ⁵ Don't believe your neighbor or trust your friend. Be careful what you say even to your wife. ⁶ In these times sons treat their fathers like fools, daughters oppose their mothers, young women quarrel with their mothers-in-law; a man's enemies are the members of his own family.

⁷ But I will watch for the Lord. I will wait confidently for God, who will save me. My God will hear me.

The Lord Brings Salvation

⁸ Our enemies have no reason to gloat over us. We have fallen, but we will rise again. We are in darkness now, but the Lord will give us light. ⁹ We have sinned against the Lord, so now we must endure his anger for a while. But in the end he will defend us and right the wrongs that have been done to us. He will bring us out to the light; we will live to see him save us. ¹⁰ Then our enemies will see this and be disgraced—the same enemies who taunted us by asking, "Where is the Lord your God?" We will see them defeated, trampled down like mud in the streets.

¹¹ People of Jerusalem, the time to rebuild the city walls is coming. At that time your territory will be enlarged. ¹² Your people will return to you from everywhere—from Assyria in the east, from Egypt in the south, from distant seas and far-off mountains. ¹³ But the earth will become a desert because of the wickedness of those who live on it.

The Lord's Compassion on Israel

¹⁴ Be a shepherd to your people, Lord, the people you have chosen. They are living alone in a wilderness that is surrounded by fertile land. Let them go and feed in the rich pastures of Bashan and Gilead, as they did long ago.

¹⁵ Work miracles for us,ⁿ Lord, as you did in the days when you brought us out of Egypt. ¹⁶ The nations will

ⁿ Work miracles for us; *Hebrew* I will work miracles for him.

"The time to rebuild the city walls." (7.11)

see this and be frustrated, in spite of all their strength. In dismay they will close their mouths and cover their ears. ¹⁷ They will crawl in the dust like snakes; they will come trembling and afraid from their fortresses. They will turn in fear to the Lord our God.

¹⁸ There is no other god like you, O Lord; you forgive the sins of your people who have survived. You do not stay angry forever, but you show us your constant love. ¹⁹ You will be merciful to us once again. You will trample our sins underfoot and send them to the bottom of the sea! ²⁰ You will show your faithfulness and constant love to your people Israel, the descendants of Abraham, as you solemnly promised our ancestors long ago.

JUSTICE NOW!

HELPS FOR READING
AND UNDERSTANDING

by Frank H. Seilhamer
edited by Hartland H. Gifford

Parish Life Press   Philadelphia

ONE
THE WORD OF THE LORD CAME . . .

A few years ago while I was visiting Boston I happened to wander into a store that displayed a wonderful collection of posters. My eye caught one hanging above the entrance which the artist had entitled, "The Making of a Prophet." It was a humorous scene depicting a scrawny lad. With his knees buckling, his mouth agape, and his eyes bulging out of his head, he was staring at a cloud suspended overhead out of which lightning was flashing.

In the center of the cloud one could make out an eye, and a voice was coming from the mist. Transfixing the newly made prophet, the voice boomed out, "Well then, my son, having said yes, how would you like to have your goose cooked now?"

While that poster and its quip do not present a verbatim account of any specific making of a prophet (at least as the Bible records it) the cartoon does sum up some of the aspects that surround the summoning of those persons. The prophetic call came from God, the message delivered was indeed the Lord's, and the position did involve goose-cooking on more than one occasion. And those to whom the call went more often than not were the most surprised persons around. For of all such folks available for such a commission God should have singled them out for so arduous and awesome a task!

We need to keep each of these aspects in mind as we study these three great prophets who lived and labored nearly 2,800 years ago. The specific backgrounds for Hosea, Amos, and Micah will be dealt with in detail in conjunction with their individual books. However, before we treat them individually it is important to take an overall look at the basic characteristics of the Old Testament prophets as a group. Individuals all, each uniquely different, there were, however, a number of similarities which they all shared and which set them apart as peculiar spokesmen for God.

Called by God

If there is one characteristic that was common to all biblical prophets it was their absolute assurance that God had called them personally into his service. The Hebrew term which we translate into English as *prophet* is *nabi.* In its root sense it means "the one who was called." In every instance that call was understood by the persons who received it to have been a divine one. When it came to the making of a prophet, no human selection committee was involved in the appointment.

As even a quick reading of their books reveals, the specific calls came to the various prophets in a variety of ways. Jeremiah, for instance, understood himself to have been ordained by God before birth to be "a prophet to the nations" (Jeremiah 1:5, Revised Standard Version). Amos, on the other hand, was a herdsman and a tender of fig trees when "ordered . . . to go and prophesy" (Amos 7:14-15). Isaiah was serving as a priest when he heard God's call for a messenger during a temple service (Isaiah 6:1-8). Hosea, a family man, received his call through his personal crisis and marital difficulties (Hosea 1:1-11).

Despite all of this diversity each prophet understood his selection to have been a divine one. The only self-made or self-determined prophets in biblical history were those who proved to be false ones. The mark of each true prophet was that he or she had a personal experience with God—though not always knee-buckling in character—that proved God had chosen him or her for the task. Hence, in a very special sense, right from the beginning the prophets understood themselves to be God's hand-picked personal messengers.

The Words of God

The prophetic utterances, likewise, were understood by them to be God's words, not the prophet's own concoctions. Although the voice did not always come to the prophets out of a cloud, they definitely were not sermons which the prophets composed and then delivered to their contemporaries in God's behalf. Time and again the prophetic speeches are introduced with such telling statements as "This is the message which the Lord gave Hosea . . ." (Hosea 1:1), "God revealed these things to [Amos] about Israel . . ." (Amos 1:1), "This is the message which the Lord gave to Micah . . ." (Micah 1:1) to verify that *God,* not the prophet, was the author of the content of what was about to be said.

Only when such divine messages were received did the true prophet speak, act, or write. In fact, there were periods of silence for all of the prophets, as the short length of most of their books attests. As Jeremiah reports, he had to wait ten days on one occasion before the Lord responded to an issue he had posed (Jeremiah 42:1-7). Indeed, one of the signs of a self-appointed, and therefore false, prophet was that he or she acted and spoke without God's appointment and prompting

(Jeremiah 14:14-15). Such antics resulted in these people giving a "lying vision, worthless divination, and the deceit of their own minds" (Jeremiah 14:14, RSV).

Radical Conservatives

The third characteristic of the prophets and their messages was that they were radically conservative ethically, socially, and theologically. Contrary to many recent opinions, the prophets were not persons who broke with their religious traditions and then challenged others to bury their heritage with them. The fact is that the prophets were staunch advocates of the religious heritage from which they sprang. They continually called upon their contemporaries to embrace and live out the values they long before had been taught by God, values which they personally had promised to incorporate in their own life-styles. It is true that the prophets were *radicals* in the core sense of the word. They drove to the *root of the issues* that confronted them in their ministry, which is what the term "radical" means. They were driven to deal with the heart of social problems, not just play with the peripheral things that surrounded them.

Moreover, the prophets did so as members of the *believing community,* calling to errant brothers and sisters who were in the same faith tradition to reform and live out their lives in line with the Word of God given through the ages. It is a mistake, therefore, to depict the prophets as wild-eyed loners standing outside of the fellowship of Israel, addressing an "alien" group hopelessly trapped by outdated "traditions." If anything, the prophets saw themselves as *belonging* to the people to whom they were called to minister.

This is an extremely important point to keep in mind in an age when we are being bombarded by individuals who would tell us that to be prophetic means setting oneself against, and apart from, the organized church or traditional faith communtiy. These individuals would have us believe that even to identify oneself as a member of that faith community is repugnant to the Lord! Such an attitude was foreign to the prophets. While thundering for change within society and individual lives, they pressed God's case as members of the religious community they were challenging. For it was that *believing community,* which for all of its warts, distortions, and failures in the past, in fact produced the very ones God called to be his prophetic messengers!

The prophets were not dropped down from heaven by parachute, nor hatched in strange lands under rocks. They arose from the people of God, where they most often had been bred, nurtured, trained, and at times even supported in their work. As they carried out their mission they drew upon the religious heritage which they shared with the people to whom God had sent them. As Micah himself pointed out when he stood and preached to the people of Israel, " . . . the Lord has told us what is good. What he requires of us is this: to do what is just, show constant love, and humbly obey our God" (Micah 6:8). Micah, like the prophetic colleagues who followed him, rarely delivered new or unfamiliar messages to his hearers. The word that God moved him and them to speak was one which most of the people had heard many times before.

What the prophets were called to do was move their people to be faithful to a common heritage which they had sworn to obey in dealing with God and each other. The prophetic challenges for the future appealed to their common traditions, traditions which God was pressing them to observe. The call for personal renewal was *radical* in its efforts to *conserve* what was best for society based upon their *experience* with God.

Lay People

A fourth characteristic of the prophets was that they generally were laypersons. Except for Moses, Isaiah, Jeremiah, and Ezekiel, all of the other prophets, as far as we know, were laypeople. Whether Hosea, Amos, and Micah continued to function in their normal trades alongside their prophetic ministries is not usually revealed in their books. Judging from the few sermons or acts contained in the writings attributed to them, it appears probably that either their prophetic occasions came at intervals during their day-to-day lives, or that their prophetic careers were confined to a few years, or even weeks, during which they left their homes and trades to speak and act for the Lord.

The Lives of the Prophets

Apparently not many of the prophets had happy lives, in the generally accepted sense of that term. Hosea's home was torn by the adultery of his wife. Amos faced opposition from the priest Amaziah, who went to the king with his charges of sedition against the prophet (Amos 7:10-17). Jeremiah was ostracized by his contemporaries, forcing him to cry out in his loneliness (Jeremiah 12:7-11). Later he was publicly humiliated, branded as a traitor, and thrust into prison for his efforts to save the nation. One of Jeremiah's contemporaries, a prophet named Uriah, fared even worse. He was put to death by King Jehoiakim, who murdered him with the royal sword for preaching essentially the same message in Jerusalem which Jeremiah himself proclaimed (Jeremiah 26:20-23). This lot of the prophets Jesus later summed up as he looked over Jerusalem during his triumphal entry into the city and wept.

> Jerusalem, Jerusalem! You kill the prophets; you stone the messengers God has sent you! How many times I wanted to put my arms around all your people, just as a hen gathers her chicks under her wings, but you would not let me! (Luke 13:34).

The lives of most of the prophets probably were difficult because the messages God delivered through them frequently placed them in opposition to their contemporaries. Being sent by God to challenge corruption among the lowly as well as the mighty often meant being met with hostility and rage. Despite this a distinguishing trait of the vast majority of biblical prophets was that they continued loving the people to whom they were sent.

With Hosea as one of their outstanding examples, the prophets tended to be forgiving and hopeful individuals even though they saw very few signs of change in the lives of the people they engaged. Their messages, as we shall see, are shot through with the optimistic call for people to remake their lives. If that call is to be taken seriously, then we must assume that the prophets believed that the people to whom they preached could in fact alter their conduct. If that were true, then the chance for changing the course of an individual life, a community, or a nation always existed no matter how depressing the situation appeared. The prophets clung doggedly to the conviction that even a badly corrupted social order had the potential of being turned around with God's help and the willingness of the people to take advantage of that chance for a new day which the Lord continually was providing for them. This is one of the main reasons why even the most gloomy of the prophets, such as some claim Amos to be, has rays of hope for a better tomorrow. Even the harsher predictions of doom are usually couched in settings of possible restoration. And it is this combination of confrontation and compassion which has kept the prophets in the forefront of our religious heritage.

Continual Value

Because these spokesmen for God all saw life without misty-eyed illusions, their value has not faded through the thousands of years that separate them from us. The situations they addressed remain with us still, in modern dress and contemporary settings. The prophets are not just figures *from* and *for* the past. They, and their modern-day successors, still are able to tap us in our consciences, nudging us to get our lives in order, individually and with one another.

TWO
LOVE AND RESPONSIBILITY
(HOSEA 1:1–3:5)

The prophecy of Hosea is intimately related to his personal experience, especially his marital relationship, yet surprisingly few details about the prophet are contained in his book. Apart from the facts that his father's name was Beeri, that he married an adulterous woman named Gomer who bore him three children, little else is revealed about Hosea. From the prophet's own statement, his ministry spans the reigns of five kings, all of whom are named in the opening lines of his prophecies. Four of them, Uzziah (783-742 B.C.), Jotham (750-735 B.C.), Ahaz (735-715 B.C.), and Hezekiah (715-687 B.C.) ruled in the southern kingdom, Judah, which had its capital in Jerusalem. The fifth, Jeroboam II (786-746 B.C.) reigned in Samaria, capital of the northern kingdom of Israel. If Hosea, indeed, remained active until the time that Hezekiah was crowned king, there is no indication of any prophecies coming from that period following the annihilation of the northern kingdom. It is hard to imagine that had he still been functioning, he would not have referred to the collapse of that realm when the Assyrian King Shalmaneser V conquered that city and subjugated the nothern kingdom in 722-721 B.C., exiling many of its citizens and resettling it with his own forces. Yet, no prophecies from Hosea seem to indicate that that calamity had struck during his lifetime.

When Hosea's prophetic career began the northern kingdom was intact. The Syrian wars which had raged during much of the ninth century B.C. had ended and a time of great national prosperity was underway. The palaces of Samaria were decked with gold and ivory, trade was flourishing, and the economy boomed. To most of Hosea's contemporaries life in their nation seemed to be on the upswing and everything was as it should be.

Beneath the veneer of this prosperity, however, injustice and corruption were rampant. The moral and ethical values which the Israelites had accepted as the people of God had been largely abandoned with disastrous consequences for the poor and weak members of the land. Oppression, theft, prostitution, and murder all had become commonplace in a nation which was able to accept them with growing callousness. The Ten Commandments which the Israelites had accepted on Mount Sinai as guidelines by which they would shape their lives together and with the Lord, had been bent so out of shape in the intervening years that they were barely recognizable. At Mount Sinai during the Exodus, the people of Israel had made promises in a covenant event, much like a marriage ceremony, in which God and people bound themselves into eternal partnership. While the Lord had kept his promises the people had thrown him over in pursuit of their own ends. "Unfaithfulness" (1:2) akin to Gomer's action in leaving Hosea, a husband who loved and longed for her, characterized Israel's leaving God behind in order to give themselves to one idol after the other as convenience served.

This shattering of the covenant bond, and the social and personal crimes which followed, formed the arena in which the prophecies of Hosea were delivered. He was sent by God to recall the nation to faithfulness to their Lord and each other. God was chasing Israel, as Hosea sought Gomer, in an attempt to rewin the people he loved after they had deserted him for others. The Book of Hosea is one long plea by God to a hardening and recalcitrant people, to turn their lives and relationships around before total destruction would befall them individually and collectively.

Hosea's Wife and Children (1:2-9)

As understood in the ancient East, in the covenantal relationship both partners committed themselves to lifelong loyalty to each other. Each party in making the covenant was made fully aware of the terms involved in the agreement (called stipulations or commandments), and the responsibilities and privileges they thereby assumed. Following that, each covenant partner personally affirmed the compact. It was a basic assumption in all covenant making, whether the agreement was made on Mount Sinai between God and the Israelites, or fashioned in a business place between colleagues in commerce, that each covenant partner was fully capable of living up to the terms or expectations of their contract. If, therefore, they broke the terms of the treaty, i.e., "sinned," then each could be held accountable to the other for their actions, being guilty of "unfaithfulness" to the partner offended.

That they were capable of living lovingly and loyally with God and each other, but did not choose to do so, formed the basis for God's charging the Israelites with waywardness. They had been "unfaithful" (1:2), the Hebrew term for which, *zanah,* means literally "to commit adultery or fornication." The Israelites had actively linked themselves with what was corrupt. The consequences of that aggressive pursuit of sin led to internal decay for the kingdom, and helpless people suffered immensely because of it. Since Hosea's wife had proven as wanton in her dealings with him as Israel had with the Lord, Gomer became an illustration for Hosea of the character of his contemporaries in relationship to God. Each of the children Gomer conceived was given a name symbolic of the condition of the northern kingdom in Hosea's time.

The first child (1:3) was named *Jezreel,* which means in Hebrew, "God sows." The name was intended to call the nation's attention to the place where Jehu had put an end to the line of King Omri by assassinating the entire royal family as punishment for the sins committed by Ahab and Jezebel (2 Kings 9–10). Just as that wickedness had been dealt with on the spot by God, the Lord again was "sowing" his plans to act in a similar manner against the evils of the incumbent king and his power structure sometime in the near future.

Hosea was told by God to name his second child *Unloved* (1:6). The Hebrew name is *Lo Ruhamah,* which can best be translated, "without deep motherly love." The Hebrew root, *rehem,* refers to the womb, which is associated with the most intense feelings of attachment. The name is a telling description of the kind of intimate relationship God and Israel had had in the past, but which had been broken by the people's defection.

The name of the third child, again chosen by God, was to be *Not-My-People* (1:8-9), in Hebrew, *lo ami.* The name is a play on the words by which the covenant with God had been made, and perhaps yearly renewed. In such ceremonies the "formula of binding," was said by each of the contracting partners in a type of oath-litany. To seal the compact the people would say, "You are my God," with the Lord responding, "You are my people." To name Gomer's second child *Not-My-People* was a declaration by God that the ties of the covenant had been cut by the nation's rejection of him.

Israel to Be Restored (1:10-2:1)

The underlying love of God continually longs for reconciliation rather than estrangement. Though the bond made at Sinai had been fractured by his people, the Lord was eager for its restoration. He had promised Abraham, in their ancient covenant, that his descendants would survive him in numbers too great to be counted (Genesis 15:5; 17:1-22). Some day in the future the people from which he was now separated God wished to have reunited with him again so that that promise could be fulfilled. Like a forgiving marriage partner dealing with a recalcitrant spouse, God refused to slam the door shut on the people he had loved for so long. One day, *Not-My-People* would again be "God's People, and *Unloved* would be once more "Loved by the Lord."

Unfaithful Gomer–Unfaithful Israel (2:2-13)

But forgiveness is not a cheap action or attitude in the biblical understanding of the term. While it is given by God freely and without condition, forgiveness can never have its real effect on persons who reject it, or who do not want it. So long as Israel preferred adultery to God (2:4-5), she remains turned away from the offer of God's mercy which he extends toward her. The inevitable consequences for such persistent stupidity are pain, suffering, and ultimate destruction (2:9-13). Eventually, most people find that when they turn their backs on God to dedicate themselves to other idols that appear more atractive, the gods to which they sell themselves become devourers, rather than saviors.

The Lord's Love for His People (2:14-23)

As Martin Luther liked to point out, "Judgment is the work of the left hand of God." His most used and powerful arm is the *right* one of mercy and salvation. In the face of the odds against success, God's plan continued to be one of pursuing the whoring wife running to her lovers, hoping to woo her back "with words of love" (2:14). As the Lord once had Israel cling to him in the wilderness when he was bringing her out of Egyptian bondage, he hoped again that the day would arrive when such a reunion and relationship would be possible.

The language of the covenant, and the marriage bond, are central to the language God speaks to Hosea. It is important to note that in his talk of passionate love, God does not mention the disloyalty of his people in shattering their union in the past. In fact, it is God who takes the initiative in these verses in attempting to reclaim his wayward people. Notice how persistently the term *I* is used in describing God's role in the repairing of that fractured relationship: "*I* will make . . . ," "*I* will be true . . . ," "*I* will show . . . constant love . . . ," ". . . *I* will keep my promise . . . " (2:19-20). The basic point being made is that even though he is the innocent party in this marriage breakup, God is the one taking the first steps toward healing the relationship, and in attempting to rehabilitate the sinners and the society involved.

This, of course, is the basic character of mercy (2:23), as God lives it out. It is a quality that moves beyond giving people what they deserve, toward giving them what loves wants them to have! Were God to deal with people on the basis of the former rather than the latter, annihilation instead of the chance for a new beginning would have been the fate of the Israelites.

Hosea and the Unfaithful Woman (3:1-5)

Like a parable in flesh, God tells Hosea to personalize the message of God's forgiving love for Israel in Hosea's own relationship to Gomer, his faithless mate. As his people were to learn time after time, that was God's way of making his point in unmistakable fashion. Love is most comprehensible when it is embodied in person-to-person acts. Jesus later was to demonstrate this when the "Word became flesh and dwelt among us" (John 1:14, RSV) demonstrating that love in its greatest degree works itself out in tangible ways. That, of course, is the goal of all religious commitment.

Hosea was called upon by God to do precisely that in his own family relationships. He agrees to buy Gomer from the ones to whom she apparently had sold herself as a prostitute. In a show of his abiding love, Hosea brings her home. He tells her that she is to live in his house but for a long time will not be allowed to have intercourse with him (3:3). In making this condition a part of her return, Hosea, in effect, was turning over a new page in their relationship, attempting to go back to the beginning of their wedded life together. For to wait a prolonged period before having sexual relations was a custom observed in the marriage of young virgins to their fiances. In such cases the potential bridegrooms had to wait twelve months after their initial commitment before the marriage could be consummated. In effect, God was prompting Hosea to treat a prostitute like an unblemished young maiden! It was the Lord's way of demonstrating that he was willing to give Israel a chance to begin again their life with a clean slate.

True forgiveness, as we shall see, involves such an attitude towards the past. Whether it comes from God to people, or from person to person, forgiveness is the willingness to let the past go and to look forward to a new day. Despite their track record, God would deal with Israel as Hosea had dealt with his wife. "The time will come when the people of Israel will once again turn to the Lord their God, and . . . receive his good gifts" (3:5).

THREE
ACCOUNTABILITY
(HOSEA 4:1—7:2)

Mercy, though it is always undeserved, is not a term interchangeable with stupidity or softheadedness. While God is portrayed by Hosea as loving and forgiving, he is also one who calls for accountability from his people.

The Lord's Accusation Against Israel (4:1-3)

This evenhanded character of God is demonstrated in these three verses. The accusation made by the Lord against the nation (4:1) is cast in the form of a court case which a prosecutor would bring against the defendant charged with a crime. The Hebrew term for such a case, *rib*, has the precise sense of filing a brief based on evidence which the wronged party has assembled.

The specific charges Hosea enumerates against the nation are largely violations of the commandments which were linked to the covenant made on Sinai (Exodus 20:1-17). Lying, murder, stealing, adultery, and the breaking of promises made under oath abounded. The agreement to observe that handful of provisions as the touchstones for their dealings with God and other human beings, had been made by the Israelites without threat or pressure on God's part during the desert journey from Egypt. The Decalogue and the covenant that embodied it were based upon a relationship of mutual love that had developed between the Lord and his people during their years together. These commandments were not bluenosed laws laid upon human beings by a heavy-handed Judge aimed at wringing all the joy out of living. Rather they were direction setters for a wholesome future shared with his people by a Creator so that they could live their lives as free individuals without destroying themselves.

Only two of the commandments are, in fact, written as "orders," i.e., in the *imperative,* in the Hebrew text. The ones referring to the Sabbath and to parents are written in that mode, and are properly translated as commands. The other eight are written in the *indicative mode* in the Hebrew text. That means that when translated they should read "You *will* not" rather than "You *shall* not" as in our English Bibles.

The key issue is that God's call to fairness, value, and respect for human dignity, and undivided loyalty to the Lord himself, was in fact evoked by him from his people, not demanded from them as some sort of duty to be done grudgingly. If the Israelites were to live as his people, then they were to worship him as Lord, making it as natural as breathing to develop a life-style with him and with each other that would reflect the love that the Lord had shown in his dealings with them. Like a truly successful marriage, love, not law, was to provide the glue that would hold the partners together. When the time came that love faded, and apathy and disdain took its place, that change showed itself in the treatment the human partners began to give to their Lord!

The trampling of the covenant provisions was proof that a total breakdown had occurred between Hosea's contemporaries and God. As is usual with sin, even the innocent begin to suffer from its effects.

So Hosea predicts "the land will dry up, and

everything that lives on it will die. All the animals and the birds—yes, even the fish—will die" (4:3).

The effects of sin have the power to knock the whole world out of balance.

The Lord Accuses the Priests and People (4:4—5:15)

The failures of the religious leadership, whose responsibility it was to teach the faith to their people as well as to be their living examples, was challenged by the Lord. Instead of being faithful to their calling, both the prophets and the priests chose to be successful, growing "rich from the sins of my people" (4:8). They encouraged moral corruption rather than condemn what was taking place. The form of unfaithfulness sins such as idolatry took was essentially sexual in origin (4:12-13). Figuratively, it involved an individual's joining himself or herself in various forms of allegiance to gods other than Yahweh. In actual practice, since many of the cults which the Israelites joined had ceremonial fertility rites, sexual intercouse was often indulged in by the devotees and the priestesses who were temple prostitutes. Some of these orgies were held on hilltops beneath the branches of trees. The trees were signs of virility, especially the pines that stayed forever green. Through these sexual relationships it was believed that the god being worshiped could be induced to follow the practitioners' example and impregnate the fields and flocks of his servants to insure prosperity for them. This abuse of other human beings in such practices and the underlying assumption that the God of Israel was promiscuous were so repugnant to God that he continually thundered against the rites wherever they appeared.

Seeing such immorality, Hosea predicted that punishment for the people was on its way (5:2). The purpose of the chastisement was going to be God's attempt to bring the nation to its senses before it destroyed itself. The Hebrew term translated *punish* in this verse is *musar.* Its essential meaning is "to teach," or "to instruct." *Musar* describes God's attempt to help set people on the right track by reeducating, and redirecting, their attitudes and their lives. One of the lessons Hosea taught through his prophecies is that the Lord is a loving teacher, not a hard-nosed vindictive taskmaster. God's goal is to make a nation which is "unfaithful . . . and unfit to worship" him (5:3) into a people who once again will resond positively to his overtures to return to their God.

Despite the desire to teach, if the evil in the people's hearts is so great that it keeps them from responding to the Lord (5:4), they they shall suffer the consequences of their stubbornness (4:16) and see their lands destroyed (5:7). If people refuse the gifts of life, then the wages of sin is death, as Paul was later to observe (Romans 6:23). No foreign allies, even with their armies, are powerful enough to ward off such inevitable judgment for apostasy when God decides to act (5:11, 13). When the Lord moves to teach a lesson to corrupted people "no one will be able to save them" (5:14).

Nevertheless, even the suffering which sin can bring on its perpetrators may be a positive factor in life. Pain has the potential to make people rethink their lives and get their mixed-up priorities in order. Often, it is only after we are flat on our backs, with no one else to turn to for help, that we finally look to God for support and strength, finding that he is ready and willing to respond. It is that hope which the prophet expresses even while his warnings of impending judgment are being pronounced (5:15).

The People Talk of Returning to the Lord (6:1−7:2)

The temptation, however, is for people to use God's willingness to forgive against him. With an almost flippant attitude (6:1-3) the Israelites seem to bank on the divine generosity working in their favor, even if their repentance for their sins is only a sham. They toss off the words lightly, in almost a singsong fashion. However, it takes more than love which "disappears as quickly as morning mist" (6:4) to demonstrate an acceptance of God's offer of renewal. "What I want from you is plain and clear: I want your *constant love* . . . I would rather have my people *know* me, than burn offerings to me" (6:5-6, italics added).

The Hebrew word translated "constant love" in verse 6 is *hesed.* It refers to a kind of love that persists through hard times as well as good ones. It is this devotion, not religious ceremony or material treasures, that God expects from his people. Without the gift of one's self, any other sacrifice or offering is worthless to him.

Hosea was aware that God's piercing eyes could penetrate even the most pious facade. God *knew* what was in the recesses of the hearts of the Israelites, and that is what led him to promise that a time for reckoning already had been placed on its calendar (6:11). Even though their words sounded apologetic he knew that they were still determined to live life as usual. That sin, added to the others, made it impossible for God to ignore the situation any longer (7:2).

FOUR
HERE, THERE, AND EVERYWHERE
(HOSEA 7:3–9:16)

The proclamation of these chapters is that sin is universal. Poor people, average people, persons like you and me, are just as responsible for the troubles of society and the world as are the rich and powerful. The shoe of sin, in other words, slips quite as readily on our foot as it does on theirs!

National Depravity (7:3-16)

This fact is quickly pointed out by God through Hosea in the first several verses of this section (7:3-7). The people deceived the king and his officers thus helping them to commit sins (7:5), just as the king and others in power had helped lead the nation astray! The acts committed by both the rulers and the ruled obviously had been carefully plotted in advance (7:6). Nowhere can anyone be found in the whole of Israel who is even willing to consider going to God for help in their sinful dilemmas (7:7). Indeed, like a "half-baked loaf of bread" (7:8), or in another popular idiom, "like a kid still wet behind the ears," the contemporaries of Hosea go running to neighboring nations looking for solutions to their moral and social problems. Israel flits from one friend to another like a silly pigeon (7:11), literally a bird whose flight is erratic because it is in the molting season. Like a frantic individual making the round of the neighborhood for quick help in a crisis, the people run from ally to ally in a frenzied search that is doomed from the start. When our sins and corruptions finally begin coming home to roost, dashing around in an attempt to deal with them ourselves is an exercise in futility. No human being can shelter us from the ultimate consequences of our deeds.

"Doomed" is the way Hosea described the effort (7:13). The sins that have been committed are of the worst kind, and punishment is on the horizon. Israel "rebelled" (7:13), in Hebrew *pasha,* against the Lord, and in so doing cut the ties with their only hope. For to be in rebellion means to want to end the relationship with the one being rebelled against, hoping in the effort to leave him or her behind, denying any previous commitment. When Hosea and the other prophets use this term to describe the actions of the people of Israel against the Lord, it is something they do almost in horror. For such an action indicates a desire to take the place of God, to assume final authority in life.

People who make such a move ultimately come to learn, sooner or later, that we human beings make very poor deities! Most of us have more than we can handle keeping our individual lives functioning smoothly from day to day. To think of attempting that minus God's help and guidance, as well as try to run the whole world on our own, is a fantasy with nightmarish potential. Such arrogance can only lead to chaos, disaster, and inevitable destruction.

The Lord Condemns Israel for Idol Worship (8:1—9:16)

Often God's punishment is meted out indirectly. Frequently the very things and persons we substitute for God and place our trust and confidence in become the agents for our grief, bringing us pain when we expected support. As pointed out in the introduction to Hosea's prophecy, he addressed his nation at a time of great material prosperity. Under no serious military threat, with trade and commerce flourishing, and no plagues or long droughts to contend with, Hosea's talk of impending calamity seemed farfetched. The manufacture and worship of idols (8:4-6) seemed harmless enough, and all their neighbors were doing it. The kings which they chose (8:4) had kept business going as usual. Even their foreign alliances had produced a period of peace. Assyria, the world's greatest power, and the Israelites had a treaty of mutual defense. In what better hands than their great military neighbor could Israel possibly place its future for safekeeping? Such a reading of the contemporary scene made Hosea's words seem to be coming from a lunatic. He not only predicted that trouble was to come for his countrymen in the near future, but that great pain would be brought to them by an Assyrain oppression (8:10).

Yet within the lifetime of many of the people who heard those predictions, the ominous warnings were fulfilled. Like lightning, the Assyrian "friend" suddenly turned into a conquering horde. When King Hoshea, ruler of Israel from 732-724 B.C., made an alliance with Egypt and withheld his tribute from Assyria (2 Kings 17:4) their former "saviors" took the offensive and, under Shalmanese V (727-722 B.C), made the predictions of Hosea come true. Samaria, the capital of Israel, was taken in 721 B.C. in a vicious battle. The people who once had "gone off to seek help from Assyria" (8:9) were exiled from their homes. "The gold bull worshiped in Samaria" was indeed "smashed to pieces" (8:6). The manufactured god in which they had placed their trust was unceremoniously carried off as a prize of war by the conquerers just as were the people who worshiped it and whom it was supposed to protect! The fire that God had predicted would destroy their palaces and cities (8:14), did in fact wipe out their fortified towns as they left for their captive land.

Such events seemed impossible when Hosea predicted them. His prophecy that "the time for punishment has come, the time when people will get what they deserve" (9:7) finally came to pass. He who was dismissed as the fool and insane man eventually was seen to be the right reader of the times. It must have been painful for Hosea to learn that those to whom he was sent with his messages of salvation turned deaf ears to his pleadings choosing destruction instead. The people indeed were "stubborn as wild donkeys" (8:9) even with the persistent prophet, and his determined God, trying to lead them away from calamity. Having experienced such recalcitrance through the ages in his dealings with the Israelites, it is not surprising that God threw up his hands saying: "Because of the evil they have done, I will drive them out of my land" (9:15).

FIVE
JUDGMENT NOW
(HOSEA 9:17—12:14)

Most of us like to think of judgment in connection with some remote point in time and involving people other than ourselves. We imagine that if the day of reckoning does occur, it will appear at some vague moment in history we label as "the end of the world." And if we go so far as to imagine who will be present for that event, it is always a "they" (not "we") who will be on hand to experience it.

Hosea was facing people with similar convictions when God sent him to preach to the Israelites. In all probability those who gathered to hear him yawned, and shifted their weight from one foot to the other, as they halfheartedly gave their attention to his sermons predicting doom. What the odd man said might someday happen, but not to them in their time they were sure!

The Prophet Speaks About Israel (9:17—10:15)

To break through to their consciousness God prompted Hosea to drum home his point about impending disaster on repeated occasions. "The God I serve will reject his people, because they have not listened to him. . . . Their hearts are deceitful, and now they must suffer for their sins" (9:17—10:2). The cutting edge of this entire section of Hosea's prophecy is carried in five words in these two verses.

The first key word in this section is *reject,* in Hebrew, *ma-as.* Its root meaning is "to despise," "to reject," "to repudiate," or "to refuse." Picture a person involved in the inspection of fruit or produce. Searching for spots or deformities that make it unfit for consumption, some pieces picked up are thrown aside on the garbage dump to complete their decay. To have God use such a concept in his dealings with the Israelites was heavy language indeed! Hosea earlier spoke of God as the "wooer," who with passionate pleas of warm affection is bent on winning back the wandering people who had deserted him (2:2, 14). But this shift in figure helps to illustrate that when attempt after attempt at wooing fails, the time eventually comes for God to leave his people to the fate they obstinately have chosen for themselves. Such a move is made only after long and intimate inspection and probing. That such a point can be reached is a warning which Hosea gave his contemporaries.

The second word, *listened,* in Hebrew *shamah,* gives the reason for God's rejection of the people. *Shamah* is a double-edged term which means "to hear" and "to obey." It accuses the residents of the northern kingdom of two cardinal sins. First, they have "tuned out" the Lord in his attempt to communicate his will for them. Second, even when they did hear him, they refused to act positively on what he asked them to do with their lives. As any parent can understand, continual pleas to children to respond to some request for action which go unheeded can lead to intense irritation. The Book of Hosea shows that God suffers when deliberately ignored. As a passionate, feeling deity, he gets weary and frustrated when confronted with rebuff and downright obstinacy. Those who will neither hear nor respond have to have other measures applied to get their attention. Sometimes the technique needed raises welts (or worse) when delivered.

The third important word in these verses is *heart,* in Hebrew *lev.* While the term usually refers to that important organ of the body, it has broader significance. For the Israelites the heart was the control center for human action. It was the heart that received, filtered, and deciphered messages. Once processed, the heart directed the course of action that was to follow. Therefore, the condition or attitude of the heart was crucial for the shaping of all relationships. If the heart was corrupt then the trend of the life it controlled would be so affected.

As the fourth key word *deceitful,* in Hebrew *chalak,* declares, it was the condition of the national and individual heart that in fact caused the ominous problems of Israel. *Chalak* describes a substance or person that is smooth and slippery, making a firm grasp difficult. It can describe a hypocrite playing one role after another as his or her current fancy dictates. The worst of this all is that it divides a person's commitments and loyalties. Where Israel was concerned, it had split her allegiance between God and other values.

Taken together, these verses form an indictment by God against the Israelites which was shattering in its import. God was ready to cast them aside because they had shown themselves unwilling even to listen to his appeal for reforming their behavior. With their individual centers of loyalty split and corrupted, they were destined to suffer for their sins and that suffering was coming not for some distant generations, but for those whose guilt had already been exposed in their own time. The lowering of the divine "boom" was not a thousand years away, but just around the corner. The hour for learning their lesson had arrived!

The fifth word in the series *suffer,* in Hebrew *asham*, carried just such a connotation. It means "to lay waste," or "to knock down." Hosea uses it to indicate that the blows God is going to administer are not going to be mere taps designed to let his people know that he is in the vicinity. When the Lord is finished the nation will be flat on its back! Hopefully, from that horizontal position, the whole kingdom will have the chance to learn from the experience and, when it passes, to arise chastened but still alive. The prediction does not imply utter annihilation. Like a loving parent, the discipline of the Lord is intended to correct, not destroy. That does not mean that the consequence of evil may not be as gruesome as the crime itself. Still, the intent of the Lord is to redeem those too headstrong to heed subtler attempts at rescue.

God's Love for His Rebellious People (11:1−12-14)

The recitation of the list of calamities in store for Israel is followed by a tender and moving hymn of love preserved for us in this section. Recalling the days when he carried and led his people much like infants through the desert after rescuing them from Egypt, God opens his heart to the nation whose punishment he has already decreed. In a series of father-child vignettes the Lord recalls how he gently tried to train the Israelites from their infancy to develop into mature and honorable men and women. Like a parent teaching a toddler to walk, he had taken them by the hand to support them in their first steps toward adulthood when they first struggled to their feet (11:3). And yet, for all of the intimacy and tenderness displayed (11:4), the response he got from the people he embraced was rejection. With the legs he had trained to walk with him, they ran in search for others to whom they could give themselves! Even divine love cannot forever hold off the consequences of such waywardness (11:7). Indeed if the love of a parent for a child is great enough, sharp jolts may have to be administered to turn that child away from a trend of life that ultimately might mean death. At moments like this, the pain inflicted needs to be seen as love's response to desperate situations.

Hosea saw God dealing with Israel in much the same way when it was heading for suicide. The God who was threatening punishment to turn them away from their sins, was the same God who had tenderly attempted to teach them to stand on their own feet. The suffering that was coming was God's passionate attempt to keep Israel from committing suicide.

The twelfth chapter of the Book of Hosea needs to be seen in this light. When viewed from this perspective it complements the opening verses of the previous chapter in this section. Neither the prophets nor God, *because of their love,* can lightly brush off the sins tearing apart their people. Though punishment will come (12:2), both are looking beyond that trauma, longing for the day of reconciliation when the Lord and his people can be together again as they had been in times past (12:9).

SIX
THEN COMES THE MORNING
(HOSEA 13:1–14:9)

Hosea saw the punishment of his people as the prelude to their restoration. While he focused clearly on the sins of the nation and their consequences, that was not his only prophetic theme. The possibility for divine forgiveness, and a chance for a new beginning, were realities he proclaimed as well. In fact, the former (punishment) was really a preliminary aimed at making the latter (divine forgiveness) occur.

With Hosea particularly, the forgiving quality of God is always uppermost. God, who calls for integrity and mercy from his people, himself demonstrates those same qualities. The God-given opportunities to separate from corruption is a fundamental underpinning of the prophet's pleas that the Israelites show loyalty for the Lord, and love and justice for each other.

Judgment and Opportunity (13:1–14:8)

Hosea reminds his hearers that "Israel's sin and guilt are on record, and the records are safely stored away" (13:12). That is, past corruption is never forgotten either by human beings or by God. When sins are committed against an individual, those painful incidents are imprinted on memory banks, there to remain for life. We seem to have been born with a kind of replay recorder built into us, where our sufferings and heartaches, as well as our joys, are caught and kept available for repeated reference. The replay mechanism can be tripped by any number of things. The name or sight of the person who hurt us, a similar incident experienced or mentioned, can cause that machine to go into operation. When it does we actually relive those blighted moments we have endured, with all of the old feelings of distress and resentment coming over us once more as though they were all happening on the spot.

The great problem the memory bank presents is that it cannot be stripped of its data. Even modern psychiatric procedures cannot erase the past in any selective and precise way. That is one of the reasons that the old proverb, "Forgive and forget" is at best only partial. If we could forget we would not have to forgive, since the event that made forgiveness necessary could be eliminated, and that would be that!

It is because we remember that we have to learn to forgive in spite of the past. Forgiveness is an act, as well as an attitude, which makes it possible for an offender to have a new chance to remake relationships despite the past which is still remembered. Forgiveness is the quality which closes the files on the sins that have gone before and then locks them shut, treating even lifelong acquaintances as though they were newborn. Forgiveness focuses on future possibilities for a chance to begin again, not on the recounting of the shortcomings of the past.

The Hebrew term for *remember, zachar,* underlines this possibility. It means literally "to count," or "to recall." It is used by the psalmist when he pleads with the Lord: "Remember not the sins of my youth" (Psalm 25:7, RSV) and by Isaiah when he pleads with God to "remember not iniquity for ever" (Isaiah 64:9, RSV). Both men were requesting that God, rather than continually enumerate their errors of the past, give them the chance to begin a new chapter in life with the pages unstained and free.

That "heaven knows" how fallible we are, is far more accurate than some people imagine. What is equally beyond most people's comprehension is the great willingness of "heaven" to put aside the mental files on our demonstrated foolishness (13:13) and rebellion against the Lord (13:16) when we become truly repentant. In a sense, God is a gambler who is willing to place high stakes on the potential for renewal in the human being. A seemingly incurable optimist, the Lord regularly takes risks on those whose previous performances would make others shun them.

That is why the call for the chance for new life goes out to the people of Israel at the beginning of Chapter 14. The characteristic challenge of God through the prophets is sounded again, "Return to the Lord your God . . ." (14:1). The Hebrew word translated "return" is *shuv*. It usually is rendered in English either as *return* or *repent*. Its root meaning is "to turn" or "to change direction." The word anticipates an about-face in the direction one's life is taking.

Note that *shuv* involves activity, as well as intention. To *turn* involves actual if not always physical movement to paths diametrically opposed to the ones previously followed. Repentance demands a change in life-style, as well as words of sorrow. As John the Baptizer puts it, "Do the things that will show that you have turned from your sins" (Matthew 3:8; Luke 3:8). Such a reversal of both attitude and action was being asked by the Lord when he challenged Israel through the prophets to "return."

This does not mean that God's will to forgive was or is conditioned by our response to his mercy. He stands ready to give us new leases on life regardless of our previous attitudes in relationships with him or each other. But, the act of gift-giving can never be completed until the gift is accepted by the recipient. One cannot give to another who continually turns his or her back, even if the one doing the giving is God! In order for forgiveness to become possible, we—at God's prompting and through the potential to do so that he lovingly built into us in the initial act of creation—must *shuv,* and turn around to face him and embrace his offer. If that is done, the reconciliation God has longed for and labored to complete can take place. Then, as outlined by Hosea in 14:2-3, the prayer and the life-style which must attend it begins to become a reality. God once again moves into the center of the lives of those who once traded him off for what they thought was security and pleasure.

If the change Hosea prays for took place, then the way for a new era would be opened (14:4-7). The nation would be enabled to "flourish like a garden and be fruitful like a vineyard" (14:7), with real prosperity for all. With such change no veneer would be required to conceal a rotting social order. With God's help, a new society marked by justice and integrity would emerge and national calamity would be averted.

A Parting Word (14:9)

Whether or not this renewal would occur rested with the people, not with God. In the final words of Hosea, God was making it clear once more that he wanted to forgive rather than punish his people.

Now the next move was theirs. If they were wise enough to seize the opportunity then all would be well for the future. If they refused, and ultimately were decimated, the tragedy that would strike them would be suicide. With his sermons preached and his personal parable lived out, Hosea left for his people and for us his parting word:

"May those who are wise understand what is written here and take it to heart" (14:9).

SEVEN
ALL IN THE BALANCES
(AMOS 1:1–3:2)

The prophet Amos was a slightly older contemporary of Hosea. According to the kings listed in his preface (1:1-2), he probably concluded his work about the time Hosea was reaching the zenith of his influence. Uzziah, the ruler of the southern kingdom Judah reigned from 783-742 B.C., and Jeroboam II ruled the northern kingdom Israel between 786-746 B.C. During the great majority of the years Amos was active, prosperity was widespread, lulling the populace into a sense of complete security and a resulting complacency and moral corruption.

Although his home was in Tekoa, a fortified town about twelve miles south of Jerusalem, Amos's prophetic ministry was directed primarily toward the northern kingdom. A common man whose occupation was that of a herdsman and a caretaker of fig trees (7:14), Amos was sent by God to preach to the sophisticated people of the capital city of Samaria. For about a generation he delivered these messages. At one point he aroused such hostility among certain leaders of the realm that charges were brought against him to the king and he was forced to return home (7:10-18). Undaunted, he continued his work concluding his ministry sometime before the kingdom fell to the Assyrian conquerers in 721 B.C.

His prophecies reveal the background of a man familiar with the elements and given to reflection. Common sights contained for him messages from God (7:1-3, 4-6, 7-9; 8:1-3; 9:1-4). His oracles and sermons are conveyed in the straightforward speech of an unaffected man. Often they fell like hammer blows on the ears of a people who were unaccustomed to being told the brutal truth.

The basic thrust of Amos's prophecies centered around his concern for social justice. The cry for fair treatment of the disadvantaged was the hallmark of most of the sermons he preached. Like the other prophets of Israel, religion for Amos was commitment lived out in day-to-day dealings with God and people. Nothing else could replace morality and decency, not even the most pious religious ceremonies, costly sacrifices, or lavish offerings. It was the former, not the latter that God demanded from his people. It was for "Justice, Now!" that God sent Amos to command his people to deliver!

God's Judgment on Israel's Neighbors (1:3—2:5)

The nations about whom Amos first prophesied are peoples that surround Israel. Syria (1:3-5) bordered it to the northeast, Philistia (1:6-8) occupied the plains to the west, the kingdom of Tyre (1:9-10) adjoined it to the immediate northwest, Edom (1:11-12) lay far to the south, separated from Israel by the southern kingdom of Judah, Ammon (1:13-15) bordered it beginning at the Jordan River to the east, Moab (2:1-3) encompassed the land south of Ammon, including in its territory much of the shore of the Dead Sea, and Judah (2:4-5) adjoined Israel directly to the south, stretching from there to the wilderness called the Negeb. Taken together, these countries encircled Israel.

The prophecies addressed to each of these nations are introduced with the identical words,

"The Lord says." The implication of this phrase is that the words which follow have come directly from the mouth of God.

Syria (1:3-5) is placed under judgement for treating the people of Gilead "with savage cruelty." What specifically this charge entails is unclear. The Hebrew text itself provides little help in understanding the sins involved. Literally, the Hebrew reads, "They have threshed Gilead with sharp implements of iron." Whether these tools were used to attack persons physically, or employed to tear up the land and crops, is not possible to determine from the manuscripts we have.

The prophecies addressed to each of these nations are introduced with the identical words, "The Lord says." The implication of this phrase is that the words which follow have come directly from the mouth of God.

Syria (1:3-5) is placed under judgement for treating the people of Gilead "with savage cruelty." What specifically this charge entails is unclear. The Hebrew text itself provides little help in understanding the sins involved. Literally, the Hebrew reads, "They have threshed Gilead with sharp implements of iron." Whether these tools were used to attack persons physically, or employed to tear up the land and crops, is not possible to determine from the manuscripts we have.

Philistia (1:6-8) is charged with carrying off a whole nation and selling them as slaves to Edom (1:6). The uprooting of an entire populace and peddling them into permanent servitude was abhorrent to the covenanted people, or should have been. While the practice of employing bonded people was common among the Israelites (Exodus 21:1-6), at the end of a seven-year period they had to be set free (Exodus 21:2). Only those who freely chose to remain in the service of their master could be indentured for life (Exodus 21:5-6).

Tyre (1:9-10) was condemned for a sin similar to that which entrapped her neighbor to the south. Like Philistia, she had carried off a whole nation (unnamed in the text) into exile in Edom, breaking a treaty in so doing. Hence, they were not only guilty of the maltreatment of other human beings, but their word had been shown to be worthless as well.

The Edomites (1:11-12) were guilty of hunting down their brethren with the sword, showing no pity or compassion. Contrary to the Today's English Version translation, there is no mention whatever in the Hebrew text that the Israelites were the persons so wronged.

Ammon (1:13-15) was even more cruel than her southern neighbors. Not only did she aggressively pursue wars of territorial expansion, but her troops went so far as to rip open the pregnant women of their captives, an act of staggering savagery.

Moab's (2:1-3) sins were of somewhat less violent nature than those of the other nations, though not less serious. They had burned the bones of the king of Edom in an act of desecration. Occasionally this kind of thing was done in order to destroy the skeletons of enemies. Reducing them to ashes, which then were made into lime for fertilizer or plaster literally wiped out any trace of the person whose being had been attached to the corpse.

The common thread that links all of these sins together is that they were violations of human beings by other human beings. God demanded a basic decency and reverence for life from all people, even those who had not made a covenant with him such as Israel had. Those who violated such norms came in for his judgement. Thus the prophet was called to speak against nations who were not part of the people the Lord had led out of slavery to make peculiarly his own.

Against Judah (2:4-5) the charges are more sweeping. The people of the southern kingdom have "despised" the Lord's "teachings" and have not kept his "commands" which he had given them at Sinai. What is more, they had embraced idolatry just as had some of their forebears. What made them so broadly condemned by the prophet was that of all of others named in his opening words of judgment, the people of Judah, God's covenant partners, should have known better than to follow such corrupt paths. They, above all, should have observed a sense of worth and dignity for all human beings in their dealings with each other.

The people of Judah knew the Ten Commandments, indeed they had pledged themselves to obey them. These had clearly outlined for them the style of life God expected them to lead. As Jesus later was to make clear, "The man to whom much is given, of him much is required" (Luke 12:48). For both the disciples of Jesus and the people of Judah the "much" referred to the knowledge of God's will as well as to material possessions.

God's Judgment on Israel (2:6—3:2)

The most specific list of grievances God has Amos deliver are the ones he brings against Israel. Their chart of offenses reads like a manual for degrading the disadvantaged and helpless society. Debtors were being sold into slavery when all they owed amounted to no more than the price of a pair of sandals (2:6). The defenseless and poor were being crushed by those with more power and wealth (2:7). Prostitution flourished as people used one another (2:7), apparently doing so in the name of God. Places of worship became houses of prostitution and usury, with human values playing second fiddle to "pleasure."

What is appalling is that the ones perpetuating the sins were those who because of their commitment to the covenant made with God had been called to be the defenders of the underdog! They had once been slaves themselves. God had freed them from Egyptian oppression and abuse. In fact, along the way to the Promised Land the Lord had counseled them to keep their past fixed firmly in mind (Exodus 22:21; 23:9), so that they would not do to others what had been done to them.

How could Israel so completely forget what oppression was like? Like many people before and after them, they inflicted on others the painful indignities they personally had experienced in the past. They should have recalled the fate suffered by the Egyptians for their oppression of the Israelites. This would have helped them to remember that their God had always taken the part of the oppressed people in the world. Not only had that been true for them, but it would be true for those who were now calling out for help. What a shock to see the Israelites becoming "pharaohs" to their own flesh and blood!

The threats that God declares through Amos are potent. The people are to feel the weight of God's anger against them just as grain shocks are crushed in an overloaded wagon (2:13). When that divine pressure comes, no one will be fast enough to escape it, or strong enough to fend it off (2:14-15). Since of all the nations on earth, the Israelites had been the ones with whom the Lord had made a compact in the wilderness, giving them special knowledge of life as it ought to be lived, therefore, of all the nations of the earth, they should expect to be held accountable for their sins.

EIGHT
BEGINNING AT HOME
(AMOS 3:3—6:14)

Is life a series of happenings without purpose or reason? In *Macbeth,* Shakespeare seems to think so when he declares that life is "A tale told by an idiot, full of sound and fury, signifying nothing." For the prophets, however, life and time were far from meaningless. All existence fits together. There was a reason for all things that occurred. And one of the organizing forces in all of life was the hand of the Lord actively participating in shaping existence in earthly, concrete ways.

The prophets never thought of God in abstract terms. He was a personal deity so close at hand that one could almost see his footprints in his world. He was not somewhere "out there," detached from his creation. Quite the opposite, he was enmeshed in the day-to-day goings on in the lives of his people.

Sometimes the divine activity seemed directed largely toward the support and encouragement of the nation. The great Exodus experience, with its miraculous release from bondage, was an ever-remembered example of that. At other times, the divine hand seemed primarily to correct and discipline those same people when they grew corrupt. This latter action was what Amos saw coming when he spoke the words recorded in these three chapters.

The Prophet's Task and Warning (3:3-8)

The God of Israel, while at times moved to anger, never was understood by the prophets as being capricious. Judgment and destruction, when they did come, were the just rewards for the sins of the people. Even in such circumstances, however, God never acted without first giving adequate warning (3:7). Amos, therefore, was prompted by God to proclaim to the nation the deluge which was going to come upon them, using as illustrations a series of metaphors drawn from the experiences of his hearers (3:3-8). Apparently, these were used to make the prophet's point because in his day and culture they would have been readily understood

The Doom of Samaria and Israel (3:9−4:13)

The specific sins of which they were guilty concerned the violation of human rights. People were cheated (3:10), the weak mistreated, and the poor oppressed (4:1). While only general indications are given in the text about the specific character of these crimes, the terms used to describe the sins themselves throw more light on their content than any other information available to us.

The Hebrew *ashak,* which is used in reference to the wrong done to the "weak," means literally "to extort," or "to handle roughly." It is a term that denotes instances where persons who have the upper hand bully or run roughshod over those unable to defend themselves. The companion accusation, is brought to the fore by the verb *ratsats*. It means "to crush" or "to shatter" and points to those events where violence done to the disenfranchised reaches levels of physical violence. Hence, even without giving us minute detail, these Hebrew words underline how desperate the situation was which confronted the common people.

With the moral climate growing worse, and the gap between the "haves" and the "have-nots" getting wider, God had decided to intervene in the situation. The "well-fed cows" (4:1) of Samaria (literally, "bullesses," women who acted as belligerently and as overbearingly as men) and their husbands would be getting their punishment from the Lord. Their land would be invaded (3:10), their lavish homes would be destroyed (3:15), and they themselves would be "roughed up" and "crushed" by others who would oppress them (4:2-3).

Note that the punishment which their deeds will bring upon them is described by Amos in very concrete terms. That punishment was to be expected within their lifetimes, not at some future date after death. These factors were part and parcel of the ancient Hebrew understanding of life and its consequences. Since they had no understanding of what later became known as "resurrection" or "life after death," justice and punishment had to take place on this side of the grave if it was ever to happen at all.

A search of the Old Testament will reveal little evidence of a well-developed doctrine of eternal life. In the older Hebraic manuscripts, the basic understanding of life after death was that one could live on only by way of his or her name being carried in the hearts and memories of others who survived.

But even if an individual didn't have children to carry on his name, he could live on by erecting a building or a monument to himself. Absalom, who had no children built a pillar that "resurrected" him in the thoughts of those who saw it. By remembering his name, they in essence brought Absalom back from the dead! Similarly, the kings of Egypt erected colossal statues of themselves and carved their names upon them. Indeed, the worst thing that could happen in ancient Israel was that somebody's name would be blotted out of the book of life. For where the name was erased, the person whose being it embodied would be forgotten, and therefore die forever.

The understanding of life after death that later emerges in the Bible did not make its first appearance among the Hebrews in its more developed form until they returned from exile in Babylon in 539 B.C. While in captivity they lived among a group known as the Zoroastrians, a Persian religious group who had a well-developed doctrine of life after death, complete with a physical resurrection. The Persians believed that a god named Ahura Mazda (the god of light) was the deity of this world and the next. At the end of time, said the Zoroastrians, there would be a great battle between the powers of good ("the sons of light") and evil ("the sons of darkness"), prior to which there would be a resurrection from the dead in which *all* persons would come out of their graves to participate in the clash. The losers in the great struggle, whom they assumed would be the "sons of darkness," would be cast into a lake of fire to be consumed. The winners, whom they were convinced would be the "sons of light," would be taken to a place known as *Paradaesos,* which was the walled garden that adjoined the palace of the Persian king. Within this garden the king sat upon his throne. Only his selected friends, his "chosen ones." were taken into this park to share the company of their master. Those who were so assembled would live with the king forever. They would pay homage and exist in peace and tranquility with him and with each other.

When the Hebrews returned from Exile, they began to include some of these religious concepts in their own faith affirmations. Their understanding of life after death included now a place called "paradise," where God would gather the righteous people after a physical resurrection. As one of the books completed after the Exile was to declare: "And many of those who sleep in the dust of the earth shall awake, some to everlasting life, and some to shame and everlasting contempt" (Daniel 12:2, RSV). This text is the first clear reference in an undisputed portion of the Old Testament to physical resurrection from the dead to eternal life. Following the Exile, it was the Pharisees among the Jews who accepted this understanding of life after death involving a resurrection, and developed its implications further. Not all Jews, however, believed that such a resurrection would occur. The Sadducees, for example, denied the reality of the experience (Matthew 22:23; Mark 12:18; 1 Corinthians 15:12). But, because of pharisaic teaching, which had tremendous influence upon the Jewish populace after the return from Exile, the resurrection from the dead, with an attendant final judgment, was a well-founded doctrine long before the time of Jesus. It is significant that Jesus himself affirmed this pharisaic position in his preaching about resurrection, and verified the truth of it by rising from the grave himself.

When Amos predicted that "the Lord God Almighty" would "punish the people of Israel for their sins" (3:14), it was with every expectation that this would occur almost immediately. God had tried through words (3:13), natural catastrophe (4:6-10), and heaven-sent destruction (4:11) to work a change and motivate repentance within the nation. Since the people still refused to "come back" to him, the time had been reached to get ready to face God's judgment (4:12).

Call to Repentance (5:1−6:14)

And yet, before he would unleash his wrath, God made still another atempt through Amos to give the Israelites a chance to avert the onslaught. "Come to me, and you will live," was the plea Amos was sent to make (5:4). "Work for what is right, not for what is evil . . . love good, see that justice prevails in the courts" (5:14-15). "Let justice flow like a stream and righteousness like a river that never goes dry" (5:24).

The sign that they had a willingness to turn their lives around would be that righteousness would become the norm for the realm. In Hebrew, *tsedekah,* means "*doing* what is right," "*acting* appropriately." Righteousness is an active term, not simply a mental exercise. It is an attitude toward others that moves one to demonstrate love and respect by fair play and honesty. It is interesting to note that where the Bible uses that term to describe individuals, they are always engaged in living out God's will for them, or caught up in acts of compassion for other human beings (Genesis 6:9; 15:6; Proverbs 10:1−11:31). Amos employs it in much the same sense when he calls for repentance. No religious festival (5:21), or material offering (5:22), or hymns sung in ceremonial gatherings (5:23) can be substituted for this essential moral response. If such an ethical turn-around does not come from the populace, then foreign armies will invade the land, putting the nation under their domination from one end to the other (6:14).

NINE
THE ALL-SEEING EYE
(AMOS 7:1–9:15)

Amos was aware that wherever he turned God was there beside him. His Lord never had to "break through" into history, whether it be the history of the world in general or of Amos in particular. No matter what he experienced, or where he might travel, God was personally involved in those moments and places. The Lord's presence seemed to fill every conceivable nook and cranny of existence.

Prophetic Visions (7:1-9)

Amos was not surprised to have God speaking to him while he was walking in the marketplace or in the fields as well as worshiping in shrines. In rather common sights he found divine messages. Three of those visions held the ominous news that widespread misery was on its way. The sight of *locusts* swarming in the air conveyed the forecast of an approaching devastation of the nation's food supply (7:1-3). Looking at a *flame* he was warned that a holocaust was going to sweep the land (7:4-6). Seeing a *plumb line* hanging next to a wall under construction (7:7-9), enabled the Lord to inform him of the divine distress over the crooked behavior of his people. Struck by the magnitude of what was to befall his contemporaries, Amos's response was to plead with God for forgiveness for the people (7:2, 5). In both of these instances, the Lord answered the request by doing just what the prophet had begged. Even though he had apparently already determined the response he wished to make to the nation's sinfulness, God reversed himself before actually implementing those designs.

The word that Amos employed in his prayer for the reprieve is *salach* (7:2). It is one of a number of Hebrew terms translated *forgive* or *forgiveness* in our English Bible. *Salach* essentially means "to send away", "to put distance between two people or objects." It is used to describe the act of forgiveness in which sins are taken and thrown away forever. One of the ways this was symbolized in the Hebrew community in Amos's day is as follows: The high priest would gather the nation together for a service of repentance and mourning. At one point in the liturgy, all the sins committed during the past year were confessed while the priest held his hands on the head of a goat. Later, as the bearer of the sins confessed over it, the goat was driven out of the city gates into the wilderness to be slain. The killing of this "scapegoat" would be the visual reminder that as the animal dies sins would be laid to rest. It was a sign to the nation that God did the same with the guilt of his people once they were willing to truly confess. In a very real way, the ceremony was a simple drama of how God dealt with his children (Leviticus 4:20; Psalm 8:5; 103:3).

Another common term for *forgiveness* is *kaphar* (Psalm 78:38; Jeremiah 18:23). Literally it means "to cover over," or "to fill in," usually with a substance of some kind. It is a builder's term often employed by those engaged in ship construction (Genesis 6:14), where it refers to the practice of caulking the hull of a boat, (i.e., filling in the gaps between the boards to enable a vessel to float and function as it was designed to). Scribes also used the term to describe their method of correcting errors in their written texts. When writing was done primarily on clay tablets, other materials having not yet been developed, mistakes could not be erased as simply as they are now. When errors occurred, the scribe obliterated it by covering it with a small pinch of new clay taken from his pot. Pressing the clay into the hole made in the tablet, with his moistened finger he would smooth over the surface, making it ready for a new word.

A third term usually translated *forgiveness* is *nasah* (Genesis 50:17; Psalm 32:1). Its root meaning is "to lift up," or "to stand on one's feet." When used to describe a situation in which forgiveness is taking place, it points to the activity of removing a burden from the back of a person, or helping an individual who has fallen to the ground to stand erect again.

Forgiveness involves an activity as well as an attitude. Forgiveness, like love, flows from person to person. Concretely, it involves shielding the present from the past, lifting away heavy loads, and enabling human beings to function freely again. When Amos pleads with the Lord to "forgive" Israel (7:2), his request has such implications attached to it. He is asking the Lord to withhold the calamity he intends to send, giving the people a chance for a "clean" future instead.

As usual God was willing to answer the prophet's request. "The Lord changed his mind and said, 'What you saw will not take place'" (7:3). And again, " . . . This will not take place either" (7:6). Thousands of times in the past he had done the same thing, hoping on every occasion that his people would use their new starts with him in positive ways.

Unfortunately, that did not happen where the northern kingdom was concerned. They chose to remain crooked (7:8), using the opportunity the Lord's forgiveness had given to multiply their sins. Therefore, the judgment had to come. Their places of worship were going to be wiped out and the line of their kings would be brought to an end (7:9). This time, God would not change his mind about loosing the destruction on the nation which they had earned with their deeds (7:8).

Amos and Amaziah (7:10-17)

The prophet's attempts to save his people from destruction met with rebuff and abuse. The leaders of the nation, who could have helped preserve the nation had they heeded the advice the Lord gave them through Amos, instead turned against the prophet with anger and hostility. Amaziah, the priest from Bethel, a major holy place for the Israelites located about ten miles north of Jerusalem, brought accusations against Amos to King Jeroboam in Samaria (7:10). He was chided to go home to his own kingdom of Judah and deliver his prophecies there (7:12-13). Undaunted, however, Amos stood his ground. He told Amaziah that the land would be conquered by foreigners and its people carried into exile. The high priest's own family would be decimated in the wake of the horror, his wife reduced to prostitution, and his children would die in the conflict itself (7:17).

Israel's Doom (8:1−9:10)

Through the sight of a basket of fruit, the Lord told Amos how imminent that event really was. The Hebrew word for the fruit Amos saw is *qayits.* It specifically denotes fruit that is picked late in the growing season. The Hebrew term for end or final time is *qets*. Through a play on these words, seeing the *qayits* sounded the note for Amos that the *qets* for his people was near. They were about to reap the harvest for the sins they had sown!

Those who had trampled the needy (8:4), cheated in the market (8:5), and enslaved people for the price of a pair of sandals (8:6) were going to get their due. Famine and thirst would sweep the land (8:11), leaving no escape (9:1-4). Those who had turned-their backs on God's pleading for change in the past were going to be helpless to escape a future filled with terror (9:4). For the Lord was going to "shake the people of Israel like grain in a sieve." He was going to "shake them among the nations to remove all who are worthless" (9:9). The punishment was going to be severe; many who heard it would die (9:4, 8). But from the divine sifting some would be saved, since not all the descendants of Jacob would be destroyed (9:8). At least a remnant would remain which God would then use to form a more faithful people for the future.

The Future Redemption of Israel (9:11-15)

It is this untiring love of God, which repeatedly has kept him from obliterating his creation, that comes through at the conclusion of Amos's prophecies. Even though the people rejected his numerous attempts to save them, God again tells Amos that one day the land will be regained, its towns rebuilt, and the people who are going to be scattered brought back. When this happens it will all be God's doing, another gift out of his seemingly endless generosity. He informs his prophet, "*I* will repair . . . *I* will rebuild . . . *I* will bring my people back to their land . . ." (9:11-14), making it plain that he is not going to desert for eternity the people he must punish. The land that soon will burn and be covered with corpses will be transformed into a garden spot where life will appear again. God promises *that* even before the fury of the punishment comes! How Amos must have shaken his head upon receiving such a divine commitment. So unspeakable a tragedy was looming, and the gift being readied for the future could be Israel's even now!

TEN
TEARS AND TROUBLE
(MICAH 1:1–3:12)

The city of Moresheth from which the prophet Micah came is situated in the rolling lowlands about twenty miles southwest of Jerusalem. If modern archaeologists are correct, the village lies near the ancient Philistine city of Gath. According to the introduction, Micah prophesied during the reigns of Jotham (750-735 B.C.), Ahaz (735-715 B.C.) and Hezekiah (715-687 B.C.), all monarchs of the southern kingdom of Judah. He was, therefore, a contemporary of both Hosea and Amos. While the ministries of the other two prophets focus on the northern kingdom, Micah's labors were confined primarily to Judah, with scattered references to Samaria. Even though they spent their lives in different parts of the land, it is surprising that Micah never refers to the words of either of his contemporaries, nor do Hosea or Amos ever mention him. Nevertheless the common threads that link these three prophets together become readily apparent in even a quick comparison of their books.

The bulk of Micah's prophecies appear to come after the destruction of the northern kingdom which took place in 721 B.C. The major thrust of his prophecies centered around the same type of problems that caused the northern kingdom's downfall, namely, the oppression of the poor. Like the other eighth-century prophets, Micah saw such behavior as a sign of moral decadence. Such oppression of the weak was glaring evidence of the total lack of faithfulness to the covenant which the nation had made with the Lord. His mission, therefore, was to call them to repentance and a change of life-style, and to warn of dire consequences should they fail to reform themselves and their social order.

A Lament for the Sins of Samaria and Jerusalem (1:2—3:12)

The cause for Micah's lament of the nation's waywardness is familiar to readers of Hosea and Amos. His opening prophetic statement takes the form of the *rib* or prophetic lawsuit made against Judah. Like a prosecuting attorney facing an offender in court, God speaks through Micah to press his case against his people indicting them for that most serious sin, rebellion against him (1:5). Idols had been set up in the land (1:7) which God had graciously given to his children for a home. The Lord had been replaced with objects of wood and stone. To these objects adopted from their pagan neighbors, the people of the Exodus were now giving their allegiance. As if this were not enough, such practices had moral structures repugnant to the Lord of Israel.

The specific sins that flowed from this apostasy are dealt with at various points in these chapters. The unifying factor is that they all lead to the degradation of one human being by another. One of the chief aberrations being practiced by the people was the stealing of land and homes from their rightful owners (2:2). Such an act, next to murder, was one of the most serious crimes one could perpetrate against another (1 Kings 21:1-3). Not only did it deprive an individual of the value of his holdings, but it in fact broke up one of the keys to family solidarity and identity. In the ancient East land and houses were part of a birth-right passed on from a father to his heirs. Land and houses were, as they still are for many Arabs in that section of the world today, carriers of the family's history and name. They were a base to which the family could return in times of need or trial. They signified the place where a man's father, and his father's father before him, had been born, labored, and finally died caring for, as well as being cared for by, the plots of earth in which they lay buried. A sense of permanence and continuity, of security and independence, developed between families and the soil. A sense of "being" was bound up with the ground and the developments that had become part of it. To rob a person of money was to violate the person, but to take away land was to steal a very part of one's history and identity.

Everywhere justice was being perverted with the social structure (3:1). The legal system which was supposed to provide fair treatment and equality for all was being used to subjugate those least able to defend themselves. Bribes were being paid (3:11). People were being trampled by vicious connivers who operated without restraint. Such a situation was disastrous in a land which had no police force, as such, to protect persons from social abuse. Taking care of kin was a family responsibility, or in the case of indenture, the master's. When an individual was stripped of support through death, distance, or destitution, the judicial system was supposed to be the one place where they could turn for help and humane treatment. Consequently, it was both frightening and dangerous to have such a system collapse. One never knew when one might find oneself alone, hounded by grabbers and finaglers.

What God called for from the people was "justice," *mishpat,* as the remedy for the situation. That Hebrew term means "to give a person his or her rights," "to render one's due." When voiced through the prophet it was God's demand that his people treat one another with absolute evenhandedness. All individuals, regardless of whether they were friends or not, countrymen or not, were to be given a "fair shake" by the courts and treated with dignity and compassion. If that failed to be done, then the nation had already begun to dig its grave.

The religious and civil leaders of the southern kingdom were called to account by Micah for their part in the problems that were rampant. They were the ones who by office and training had the responsibility to keep the nation on an even keel. But both apparently had sold out, or been bought up, in one way or another. They added to the problem instead of being part of its solution. Prophets lied and peddled promises of prosperity or doom depending on the ability and willingness of those who consulted them to pay for their oracles (2:11; 3:5). The rulers of the land had reversed their system of values, so that they loved corruption and despised virtue (3:1-4). "Money talked" from one end of society to the other for those who had it. But what all of the leaders forgot was that the Lord had ears to hear the "conversation" which they and their wealth were carrying on! And when the Lord got the message he moved through Micah to respond to it.

Just as Samaria's sins had brought it destruction (1:9), the same was predicted to happen to Judah and Jerusalem (1:9). Going naked and barefoot through the streets of Jerusalem to dramatize his message, Micah delivered a fateful prophecy to the inhabitants of the nation's capital. To their startled ears came the thunderous proclamation:

" . . . Zion will be plowed like a field, Jerusalem will become a pile of ruins, and the temple hill will become a forest" (3:12).

The oracle so shook his hearers that in the days of Jeremiah, nearly a century later, it was still remembered and people who walked Jerusalem's streets shuddered (Jeremiah 26:18). Though the prophecy shocked them, the response Micah got was not one of remorse from his hearers. Much as Amaziah had blazed away at Amos (Amos 7:12-13), the people of Jerusalem told Micah to hold his tongue as well:

"Don't preach at us. Don't preach about all that. God is not going to disgrace us. . . . Has the Lord lost his patience? Would he really do such things?" (2:6-7).

Despite his best efforts at driving his point home, they refused to accept the posibility that the divine patience could ever wear thin!

Quite likely the false prophets who only told the people what they wanted to hear may have done much to create the climate of disbelief and amazement which greeted Micah. These prophets not only supported the policies and practices going on, but provided asurance that God was at ease and satisfied with life as it was (2:11; 3:5, 11). When the people were confronted by a prophet of a different stripe, his word they were willing to discount. Like many of the true prophets of God, Micah had to contend with this predicament. Yet he alone, among those on the scene, was able to see with clarity what the true situation and state of the nation was. Prodded by his perceptions, he was moved to speak the truth without regard to the consequences. With the courage supplied by the Lord (3:8), he continued to call a spade a spade, even if the sermons frightened and hurt the people he confronted. His willingness to do so was evidence of the great love he held for his people. That love made it impossible for him to watch them die without making an attempt to rescue them.

ELEVEN
RUIN AND RESTORATION
(MICAH 4:1–5:15)

As we have seen in the preaching of the other prophets, *redemption* is one of their most powerful and consistent themes. They hardly finished thundering the Lord's judgment on their contemporaries when in almost the next breath they begin to preach about the possibility for a new chance at remaking the future through the mercy and with the help of God! This is especially true of the preaching of Micah. Though he often is sent by God to expose the sins of his people, threatening ominous consequences should they fail to turn their lives around, he is used by the Lord almost as frequently to deliver messages of hope. Hence, in Micah, the twin roles of God as *judge* and *savior* are constantly kept moving back and forth before his people as the prophet first thunders indict‑ments for moral corruption, then follows with assurances of reconciliation and reunion to take place sometime in the future.

The Lord's Universal Reign of Peace (4:1–5:5)

The announcement of Jerusalem's utter destruction (3:12) must have been ringing in their ears still when Micah went back to the inhabitants of Jerusalem with the announcement that annihilation of the nation was not God's intention. The day would come when out of the ruins, the city would again arise and become for the Israelites and the other nations of the world a meeting place where God would await them all as they flowed in a stream toward him and toward one another. This beautiful vision of Micah is duplicated almost verbatim in the Book of Isaiah (Isaiah 2:2-4), the great prophet who preached in the southern kingdom about the same time as did Micah. In both instances the prophecy has three major points to make.

The first is that the hilltop known as Mount Zion, which includes the main Temple complex and its court area, and which Micah declares is going to be made desolate (3:12), will be restored and God will be in residence there once again (4:1-3) The presence of the Lord in his house will be a sign that he and his people are living in harmony once more.

Second, the people of Israel and many other nations will freely come to learn God's will for them and will trust him to be their savior in time of stress and trouble (4:3). One of the charges Hosea had lodged against the people was that, forsaking Yahweh, they sought such strength and help from human sources (Hosea 7:11; 8:9). In the restoration, the people of Israel would not only be willing to hear the Lord's teaching, but would actively seek it out. Their numbers would be enlarged, since the nations whose aid they once sought, would now search with them for the Lord. It would be a uniting of many elements of the Lord's creation under his kingship.

The third point made is that, as the result of this new attitude toward God and in allegiance to him, wars would cease and the implements of battle refashioned into tools of peaceful occupation. In an exact reversal of the process recorded in Joel 3:10, Micah proclaims:

> . . . They will hammer their swords into
> plows, and their spears into pruning knives.
> Nations will never again go to war, never

prepare for war again. Everyone will live in peace among his own vineyards and fig trees, and no one will make him afraid. The Lord Almighty has promised this (4:3-4).

What the Lord is proclaiming through Micah is that following the painful calamity which the people's sins will bring upon them, an era of true peace will be ushered in for all people. While the Today's English Version arbitrarily inserts in this beautiful passage the clause, "Everyone will live in peace," these words do not exist in the ancient Hebrew texts.

The word they supply here, *peace,* is derived from the Hebrew root, *shalom.* While Micah himself does not use the word, it precisely describes what he had envisioned with his prophecy. The "days to come" (4:1) would have the world and his people living in the condition that God intended for them from the beginning. This is what the word *shalom* actually tries to describe.

"Peace" as we often think of it is too weak a rendering of *shalom. Shalom* itself comes from an older Semitic word, *salamu,* which means "for things to be complete, in perfect working order." Unfortunately, when we use the term *peace* we are often referring to what should be described more accurately as an armistice. The term is employed to describe a suspension of hostilities, even though the situation between peoples or nations is anything but in "perfect working order!" Two armies can be arranged in battle lines a mile apart, even planning future battles if they are convinced they can win, and yet since no shots are flying at the moment, the situation may be described as "peace." Or, members of a family can live in the same home refusing to talk to one another, unable to share with each other, perhaps even despising each other, and yet since no arguing is overheard and no screaming and shouting echo through the halls, that can sometimes get the label of "peace."

Shalom, however, never really fits such situations. To apply this term, hostility must truly cease, and those involved relate to one another as caring human beings. Each must see the other as belonging to a family created by God, acknowledge him as Lord, and be willing to try to live together as he intended. Only then, with real love and respect between the parties, can a state of real peace, true *shalom,* ever be seen to prevail.

In this magnificent prophecy in the fourth chapter of his book, Micah envisions such a day actually occurring. He declares that beyond the suffering and pain which sin will cause for his nation, the day will come (4:1) when with God's help a new garden of Eden will exist again. When that vision will be realized is not revealed. He leaves us with the simple assurance, "The Lord Almighty has promised this" (4:4).

Micah does not promise his people that easy days are ahead. Just the opposite is true. Their land will be leveled (4:11), pain like that of women in childbirth will come upon them (4:10). Nevertheless, some day in the future God will bring back his people from the exile they are going to experience as part of their punishment (4:6). They will go to Babylon for a time, but the Lord will eventually save them from their enemies (4:10-11). A new leader will be raised up to rule over them, replacing the king whose line will be lost when the nation is overrun.

The new leader for the future will come from the city of Bethlehem, the town that had been the home of the great King David. His family tree will reach back into ancient times (5:2). His birth will be the occasion for God's reuniting with the nation, and it will usher in the regrouping of the exiles from the places where they have been scattered. Then, under his reign, the people will live in safety. He will be the one who will bring in the *shalom* which the Lord has promised to his people (5:5). Though nothing will alleviate the fury of the chastisement in their immediate future, what a magnificent hope this promise of God through Micah holds out for his people for the days beyond the coming grief.

TWELVE
A CASE IN POINT
(MICAH 6:1–7:20)

The justice of God was never doubted by the prophets. Even in his moments of greatest wrath they saw God as merely giving people what they deserved! And those occasions came only after all else had failed. Usually God tried kinder and more tender ways to deal with his nation. Long series of warnings, and often pleadings, always preceded any pain-bringing actions. This was true in the days preceding the destruction of both the northern and the southern kingdoms.

The Lord's Case Against Israel (6:1–7:7)

In an almost last-ditch attempt to avoid the destruction of Judah, God again pleaded his case, outlining the ways open to prevent imminent disaster. God begins by enumerating the events from the nation's history which demonstrated how far he had gone to save and assist his people at important junctions in their lives. As he does so God calls on nature itself, the mountains and the "foundations of the earth," to listen to his case and act as jury (6:1-2).

The Lord opens his case by recalling the greatest of all saving events he performed for the Israelites, the Exodus experience through which he freed them from Egyptian bondage (6:3-4). He follows that by reminding them of how when Balak, King of Moab, tried to employ Balaam to put a curse on the Israelites (6:5a). The Lord sent his angel to stop him (Numbers 22:1–24:25). He goes on (6:5b) to refresh their memories about how he had dried up the waters of the Jordan River, in a type of second sea crossing when it loomed as a barrier to his people's entry into the Promised Land as they moved toward Gilgal under Joshua's leadership (Joshua 3–4.) All of these were wondrous events which no human being could have accomplished, but which the Lord had done to save the nation.

As the response to that mercy and love, God did not ask for burnt offerings (6:6), the gifts of sheep or oil, or the sacrifices of children (6:9). What he requested from his people was the life-style which he had shown them would be "good," in Hebrew *tov,* "snaped according to God's design." That shape was quite simple in its requirements:

"To do what is just, show constant love,
    and humbly obey our God" (6:8).

The requirement of justice, in Hebrew *mishpat,* meant, "to give every person his or her rights and due." It involved a determination to treat people with absolute fairness, regardless of one's personal feelings about, or relationship to, the individual in question. Persons who received such treatment did not have to bow and scrape for or because of it. In fact, they did not even have to offer thanks for it, since such treatment was theirs by right, being a creation of God. Their worth and dignity were to be respected by others, especially if those others had learned from the Lord the sanctity of all human life, as the covenant entailed.

Hesed was expected by God from his people as well. Often translated "constant love," "steadfast love," or "unending love," this Hebrew term actually means "a dogged, determined, unwilling-to-let-go, unable-to-wear-out, won't-say-quit kind of love!" No single English word can capture it completely. It is a term wrapped up with the covenant relationship between God and Israel in which each promise life long loyalty. *Hesed* expressed a determination to live out that commitment.

"Humble obedience" was assumed by God from his people, too. *Tsanah,* the Hebrew word that stands behind the English rendering, means "to keep up," "to stay in step" with the pace set by the fellow traveler. It does not mean to walk in the attitude of a beaten spirit. It has no connotation of subjugation. Rather, it depicts a person hustling to match a rate of travel that he or she might find a challenge!

What *tsanah* was asking from the people of Judah was that they act toward God and their compatriots with the same love and concern the Lord had shown them. "Match me, step for step, style for style in our relationship," is what God was saying through his prophets. Yahweh was not a Lord who demanded that people do what they were told. He always asked that they do as he did, patterning their lives after his. When he called them, "My people," they answered him, "My God." They entered into an intimate bond with him that linked each to the other. They were to follow in his moral and ethical footsteps throughout their lives.

Such an attitude, and the behavior it produced, Micah declared to be "wise" (6:9). The rejection of both not only was foolish, but ultimately disastrous, bringing "ruin and destruction" (6:13), as Omri and his son Ahab, kings of the northern realm learned. (1 Kings 16:25–21:24). If they chose to continue despite God's generous acts in saving and sustaining them in the past and his pleadings and efforts to turn them from their increasingly corrupt ways in the present, then the people of Judah were giving God no other option than to declare, "It's hopeless! . . . There is not an honest man left in the land, no one loyal to God" (7:1-2). That is precisely what the headstrong people seemed determined to do. Their course apparently settled, the day for their punishment was just over the horizon. Now, apparently alone among the people of Judah in his desire to serve his God, Micah probably shook his head as he turned away saying, "But I will watch for the Lord. I will wait confidently for God, who will save me. My God will hear me" (7:7).

God's Compassion and Promise of Salvation (7:8-20)

God's concluding words are ones of hope and future restoration. He who had predicted that ". . . Zion will be plowed like a field, Jerusalem will become a pile of ruins, and the temple hill will become a forest" (3:12), now says, "People of Jerusalem, the time to rebuild the city walls is coming. At the time your territory will be enlarged. Your people will return to you from everywhere . . ." (7:11-12). Even through the clouds of the gathering storm, the compassion of God shines!

Micah himself banked on God holding firm for the future. The final seven verses of his book are a prayer to the Lord to remain the shepherd of his people, to lead them through the "wilderness" into which they had strayed (7:14). He asks for another series of "mighty works," similar to the events of the Exodus (7:15). Forgiveness, *nasah* would be necessary for that to take place, but he was convinced that God does not "stay angry forever"

(7:18). The divine mercy would surface again, and his faithfulness and *hesed* would not fail (7:20). Micah could face the future with confidence. With God standing by, his people could endure any disaster without descending into total despair. Beyond the suffering they would encounter, God would be waiting to embrace them anew.

THIRTEEN
THE TIME IS NOW

Now that we have looked at the work and words of these three great prophets of the Lord, what ongoing value do they have for us? If their messages had been pertinent only to their own generation, we probably would never have known that they lived. But because their preaching and insights reach so deeply into the times, trials, and aspirations of millions of people born long after they died, the records of their sermons and oracles have remained alive and active to our day. Why?

Perceptive Evaluators

For one thing, these prophets have shown themselves to be perceptive evaluators of existence. Hosea, Amos, and Micah saw and reported life and people critically and candidly, pointing out issues universal and everlasting in their scope and duration. People's inhumanity to people, the blatant disregard of the dignity and rights of others, seem always to be with us. Simply change the historical, geographical, and cultural settings of the people involved, and the society and events these three prophets describe could well be our own. Practices which deny rights to minorities, be they women, people of color and race other than our own, or the economically weak and depressed, are major tragedies with which we are still struggling in this day and age. The subversion and misuse of legal systems so that "justice" seems to keep at least one eye open as she manipulates the scales, is something we read about in our morning newspapers, as well as in the books of these three prophets. The

132

violent use of power and wealth are still with us.
The shattering experience these three men of God
had in struggling with such issues makes the prophets and their works as up-to-date at this evening's
newcast!

Life As It Should Be

Another reason why these prophets remain
important for us, is that they give us keys to living
life as God intended that it should be lived. They
pinpoint for us justice, righteousnes, truth, and
continuing love as the foundations upon which we
must build our moral structures if *shalom* is ever to
be realized. Though we all long for that kind of
peace, the prophets remind us that there are no
easy avenues to its achievement. Life is complex,
and to bring wholeness and true prosperity into it,
is not something that can be done simply or without sacrifice and discipline. Hosea, Amos, and
Micah understood that. When they called their contemporaries to live the values God had shown them
in the words of life we call the Commandments,
they knew that it would involve persons giving up
substantial parts of themselves in the process. They
learned through experience, that if everyone seeks
only her or his personal gratification, then the
inevitable result for the entire social order is chaos
and pain. Families, communities, and entire
nations will collapse under the weight of the
oppression such life-styles produce. The only path
to true community is reached through a morality
that involves self-giving, discipline, and a goal
beyond immediate gratification. It means a life-
style that has as its very heart the preservation of
the worth and dignity of all human beings, and the
willingness to give every person his or her due.

That is why such words as *mishpat,* "to deal evenhandedly"; *tsanah,* to keep in step with God '; and *hesed,* "a love and respect for each other that hangs in there through good times and bad" are terms that keep reappearing throughout the prophetic books. While they are difficult to uphold, as anyone who has ever tried to live up to them has learned, without them individuals and society are doomed. We who are seeking today to build a world where we can stop devouring one another, can find in these perceptive men from the past the basic building blocks we, too, must employ if we ever are to make that dream a reality. The prophets do us a service by making us realize that such a goal is painfully hard, though with God's help, possible to achieve.

Belief in the Ability to Change

A third element that has kept the prophets plugged into the lives of the generations that followed them is their confidence in the potential for change in every human being. No matter how corrupt the persons to whom they came to preach, or how frequently their messages seemed to fall on deaf ears, they doggedly clung to the conviction that the people they addressed had the power to be better, if they so chose. Without such a conviction the preaching of the prophets would have been a farce. Their challenge to their hearers to give up their sins, and their threatening them with punishment if they refused, were based on a positive anthropology. That is, to make such an appeal, they had to be working on the assumption that the persons they called to order could meet the challenge.

When Hosea, Amos, and Micah thundered that

the Lord was demanding that Israel turn from idolatry, adultery, theft, lying, and murder, they and the Lord seriously expected Israel's compliance. The covenant God made with Israel was based on the assumption that the life-style outlined in the Commandments could be observed. Threats of punishment for failure to live up to those agreed on standards were included in the provisions themselves (Exodus 20:5-6, 12). It was precisely because the people had the potential to use these principles to shape their behavior that the Lord promised punishment should they be ignored. Even Jesus later was to base his teachings on much the same faith in the people he met. His great commandment that the disciples love one another as he had loved them (John 15:12) demonstrates his own belief that his friends were capable of a more positive style of living than they themselves may have ever imagined!

In a world where so much is said and done that undercuts a sense of positive potential in human beings, the prophetic faith in our power "to become" is good news, even if frequently it was voiced in conjunction with criticisms of backsliding and errant behavior. The prophets continually kept in mind the fact that God had built into each human being the potential to love and serve and to live creatively with others. That potential was a gift from our gracious Creator. Though often ignored and subverted, that divine gift remained available. This is one of the reasons the prophets continued to preach about the chance for renewal being offered by God in the face of apparently insurmountable odds.

That faith kept them going back time and time again to plead with their people to reverse the trends of their lives and reshape their world. That persistent affirmation still touches a responsive chord in those who wish to believe that they and other like-minded persons can fashion a tomorrow better than their yesterdays.

Hope for a New Start

Fourth, the prophets were able to extend a hope for the reconstruction of even corrupt nations. No matter how bleak the past, a new start was always possible. Even when met personally with hate and rejection all three of our prophets had as their ultimate word that God would renew his people. That held true even when the entire social structure seemed ready to collapse around their ears. Beyond the threats for chastisement, God's continuing promise was heard. He would not "remain angry forever." Corruption could be rampant and sin pervasive, but still the prophets stood firm in their conviction that the world they witnessed could be renewed. Pain, suffering, isolation, and destruction might well be part of that rebirth. But the willingness and power of God to accomplish it was something the prophets never ceased believing in.

Trust in God

The prophets never doubted either the existence of God or the absolute reliability of his word. They had met him personally in their own lives, and had experienced the results of his power. Since he continued to be present and active in his world, working in it with intensity and compassion, they remained convinced that the Lord would never abandon it in any ultimate sense. Regardless of how human beings might act, the day would come when the Lord would reshape and refashion things anew. That allowed them to hope for the coming of a new era even while foreign armies were marching toward their borders to devastate their country.

For oppressed, hurt, lonely, worn-out, frustrated, and frantic people the prophets' belief in the coming of a new era was good news indeed. It kept them alive, waiting, and believing in times of personal and national calamity. It buoyed them up when life seemed out of control and they appeared helpless.

Hosea, Amos, and Micah provided the glimpse into the future that helped them see light at the end of the tunnel of despair. They were able to do the same for later generations confronted with their own complex of problems seemingly beyond any possibility of solution. Even more pertinent, they provide us with a faith and encouragement to move forward toward personal and collective renewal, knowing that with the help of God a new day may be dawning.